IMAGINAL REMEMBERING

Our Soul's Journey

Through Memory and Imagination

DAPHNE DODSON, PhD

ISBN-10: 0998085111
ISBN-13: 978-0998085111

Cover photography and design: Jennifer Leigh Selig
(www.jenniferleighselig.com)

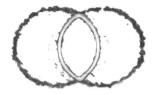

MANDORLA BOOKS
CARPINTERIA, CA
WWW.MANDORLABOOKS.COM

DEDICATION

This book is dedicated to my mom who taught me as a child how to imagine and to Nancy who reminded me as an adult that I still could and should . . . to the courageous souls who shared with me their precious memories and invited me on their imaginal remembering journeys . . . to Jennifer who tirelessly cajoled me to write with flesh on the bones . . . and to Josh, Jillian, and Dan who fill my psyche with the sweetest memory-images.

Whatever is in memory
is also in the soul.

~ St. Augustine, *Confessions*

How sweet the silent backward tracings!
The wanderings as in dreams—
the meditation of old times resumed—
their loves, joys, persons, voyages.

~ Walt Whitman, *Leaves of Grass*

TABLE OF CONTENTS

CHAPTER 1

IMAGINAL REMEMBERING:
A WORK OF AND FOR THE SOUL

I was no older than three. We lived in a small home, made with papier-mâché interior walls, in a southern Missouri town, until I turned four and moved in with my grandmother. In that town, my mom worked part-time as a receptionist and my dad as a mechanic at the local tire store. In this way, they made ends meet while he studied engineering on the GI bill at the town's state university.

I still, plain as day, see the memory in my mind's eye…I am riding a tricycle and stop at the open window where Mama stands at the kitchen sink, washing dishes. I hand her a saved tab from a bandage, the plastic part that keeps the bandage from sticking to what it isn't supposed to before it's placed near the injured skin. She smiles; yellow curtains, moved by the breeze that keeps the morning air fresh, flutter by her face. "Thank you, ma'am," she says, accepting the ticket as payment for driving on this imaginary tollway. I curve the front tire to the left, making my way back to the other end of the cement front porch that runs the full length of my home.

I can't think about that memory without a rush of joy. I doubt any childhood is perfect, certainly not mine, but this memory reminds me of how sweet life can be. How morning is a time of forgiveness for wrongs of the evening past. How a rundown home is a palace when chosen to be seen that way. How a saved piece of plastic can connect two people when they both share a willingness and courage to imagine. In this memory, I re-experience my mother's grace and lovingness that provided my frolicking imagination with just enough space to neither limit it nor let it venture too far.

I know in my heart this memory lives inside of me. I tell you honestly, this is what I believe: memory is not some objective recording, an exact replica of an actual event, etched into brain matter. The contents of our memory exist within us as that vast landscape called the psyche that holds both what is known and unknown, what is personal and transpersonal. I'd swear we can engage with at least some of our memories imaginally if we have the openness to meet them there. It's happened before my very eyes, stories I want to share with you. Maybe then you too will see imaginal remembering is a work of and for the soul.

Despite extensive research, memory remains enigmatic, often discussed but never unequivocally unraveled. Memories shape who we are as individuals and often hold significant influence on how we function within and as a community. As a research psychologist, I have witnessed memory's apparent formation of prevailing behaviors and attitudes. Asking someone a question about her present regularly results in a response that is rooted in her recent or long-term past. We often explain why we are who we are, doing what we do, by articulating aspects of our remembered history. In these ways, we seem to understand innately the value of memory as related to how we function in the world.

Why is it then that we so limit our memories, thinking of them as fixed, if not precise, objective rather than subjective? I admit to having bristled at another's retelling of a shared past when it was told differently than how it exists as my memory. That our recollections conflicted challenged my relatedness to the event and even to the other whose account differed from mine. In part, I believe this has something to do with a cultural attitude toward memory. Because we live in a culture that privileges what is measurable and thereby objectified, it seems we are inclined to grant ourselves permission to be affected by memory only if we see it as an irrefutable, historical phenomenon. Even if we might wish otherwise, this attitude seems to contribute to a memory's continual shaping of our psyche (that elusive entity seemingly charged with governing, consciously and unconsciously, our thoughts, emotions, and behaviors).

Over my years as a researcher, I have become increasingly sensitive to the notion that much dialogue occurs beyond what is conscious to the ego (that aspect of the psyche with which we currently most identify). Once upon a time, I excavated the dialogue of research interviews as if they were empirically precise and measurable. Now, I perceive these exchanges as images, as what participants want me to see because they are images in their mind's eye. Their shared memories are, for me, no longer accurate accounts of bygone events; rather, they are that which is presently imagined as having occurred in the past. I see them as images that hold the capacity to shift along with our psychological responses to them.

I also suspect these images of our psyche, or psychic images, are living and embodied—animate and autonomous. To be clear, when I use the terms *living* and *embodied*, I do not mean these images are of the same material form as that which we experience in the physical world. These living and embodied qualities should not be confused as suggesting something corporeal, like my little dog who pushes her nose beneath my hand as I try to type these words.

Rather, these psychic images are *living* because they have a life quite beyond the control of the ego. We need only look to our dreams to recognize such separation. That our waking, egoic self may be quite astonished, entertained, or horrified by what has surfaced during slumber or in daydream strongly suggests that the ego has precious little to do with these images or the actions they take during dreamtime. They are *embodied* if for no other reason than because our psychical realities are tightly interwoven with our physical realities, namely with our bodies that *embody* many unconscious aspects of the psyche, most certainly to include remnants of lived experiences.

Do you remember that front porch, tricycle, and mama standing at the yellow curtained window of my memory? When returning to that memory imaginally, these images have met me. Once, a ladybug landed on that curtain, and I watched its wings flutter before it flew to a handlebar of that red trike. Do I mean that this ladybug is living—that when I opened my eyes, I saw it and felt its tiny legs crawling on my fleshy hand? Certainly not. But I do believe it was animate and autonomous from my ego, for why else would I have been perplexed and amused by its presence? I have no conscious awareness of moving this tiny, red creature from the dancing yellow curtain to a shiny handlebar. But I do recall that its movement prompted my imaginal movement toward the scrubby front yard of my childhood home. In doing so, I re-membered, pieced back together, a time when I equally trusted things physically real and things imaginatively real, recognizing each as valuable. It might be interesting to know the ladybug, as a member of the beetle family, symbolizes a great many things. Peculiarly, this red beetle is associated to life energy and rebirth, and "an unconscious that propels consciousness into its awakenings."[1] I have pondered motives for the ladybug's appearance, never arriving at a definitive reason.

I'll tell you one apparent upside of accepting these psychic images as animate and autonomous—it frees us from the constant drive and associated judgement to interpret their meaning in terms of what they suggest about our ego. Rather, by seeing them as animate and autonomous, we come to meet them in a way that invites and accepts that their presence alone may offer essential and extraordinary wisdom and healing for us and perhaps *others* in our lives, regardless of whether these others are human or non-human.

In Chapter 6, you will meet Jennifer (all the folks you will meet throughout these stories are identified by a pseudonym) who imaginally engaged a memory of a time she ran away as a child. In the memory-image, though not in the original memory, Jennifer observed a doe and realized something of great importance to herself and the natural world—we may come to rely on what does not serve us regardless of the best intentions of such offering and receiving.

Deeply knowing who we are, personally transforming and healing, acknowledging and engaging with the creativity and the sacred within each of us: these reasons compelled me to investigate how engaging with memories as animate and autonomous images might meaningfully impact an individual's psychology or sense of self, that part of us that recognizes our own ability to reflect upon our world and our own mental status.

How then does one engage with their memories in this way? I use the term *imaginal remembering* to describe the specific process that is discussed in the subsequent chapters of this book. This practice of imaginal remembering follows the guidance of Dream Tending (as is further unpacked in Chapter 4) that subscribes to a psyche-centered approach to dream images.[2] In this way, Dream Tending extends concepts developed by the depth psychologists Sigmund Freud and C.G. Jung. The dream is first met by the technique of association (taking current personal material and making free-associations to the symbols or signs of the dreams) and then amplification (drawing upon religion, folklore, myth, art, and other historic and cultural symbols to help interpret the dream). The third step, animation, invites the dream figures (or psychic images) into the psychic field of the dreamer and the dream-tender (a guide who, through questioning, encouragement of actions taken by the dreamer, and supportive presence, helps navigate the dreamer's engagement with the images).

Recognized as autonomous beings, these images (which may also include figures that might otherwise be considered inert matter), are, with care and respect, engaged in a dialogue (spoken or unspoken) such that the dreamer meets them again, possibly more enlightened by their return visit. In this encounter, the dreamer may observe and interact with but never directs the images for they are understood to be animate and autonomous, possessing and acting upon their own intrinsic purpose.

In Chapter 6, you will meet Aria and a notebook that appears at the kitchen table of her memory-image. Why it suddenly appeared there, when we later learn this notebook (in the physical world) was lost and otherwise forgotten, is difficult to know. What Aria knows, though, is in the soft, white pages of that notebook she found the tracings of rosemary leaves and forget-me-not blossoms that whisked her away to her grandmother's homestead and led her on a journey of the self, both yesterday's and today's. The notebook seemed to have some purpose in its sudden and uncanny appearance. The truth remains, that despite what's presented as analysis of such symbolism, it is likely that neither I nor Aria will ever know the notebook's true purpose for turning up on that imaginal table in that imaginal kitchen.

The belief that memory-images may be animate and autonomous from the ego who remembers them is not meant to suggest that our memories are not profoundly real and personal, carrying tremendous affect that may shape who we are as individuals and how we carry out our lives. On the contrary, my desire to work with memories as living images emerges from my intense belief in the power and value of memory. Seeing memories as animate, autonomous images that may reshape of their own accord is not in any way to deny the actuality of the original event. The way in which an imaginal remembering experience unfolds does not imply how the historical event originally occurred. Rather, this experience, at its essence, accepts the images as communication with and from the psyche.

The first half of this book is a background, a *defense* as to why and how we might think of and then engage with our memories imaginally. Chapter 2 is dedicated to exploring past and current perspectives of memory theory with an eye towards seeing how our memories may be psychic images. This chapter is for the skeptic who still managed to read this far. With a critical sideways glance, you question the seemingly preposterous things that I suggest.

Precisely, I might say to you with a nod, for etymologically *preposterous* means reversing things, taking the *post* and making it the *pre*. You see then, I would say, we're reversing things, turning memories back upon themselves so that we no longer confine our relationship to them as strict representations of the past. Rather, we come to welcome them as invited guests who share something of our todays and our tomorrows. I might also acknowledge that you and I have grown up in a society that habitually accepts only that which is empirical, measurable, generalizable, and thus predictable. It's a bit unsettling to step outside of cultural norms—the road less traveled, the ground not well worn.

If you are this skeptical reader, you might find value in reviewing the perspectives of modern and acclaimed psychologists and neuroscientists who seem to turn such skepticism towards our culture's approach to memory. I suspect you'll be awed by their breadcrumbs-path which links memory to imagination. If you came to this book as a believer, you too might like this chapter, for it may bolster a trust in yourself as you begin to personally dabble in imaginal remembering. From my experience, it can be quite astonishing, thus easy to deny or dismiss the uncanny truths such experiences into the imaginal may offer.

Chapter 3 is dedicated to exploring the notion that psychic images are indeed living images. In their animation and autonomy, and our approach to them as such, we may be engaging with the deepest aspects of our selves to include the spirit and soul within each of us. Chapter 4 offers an approach to working with these images of our psyche. There, we explore approaching the psychic image, at first considering the phenomenology-of-the-image as a study of encountering our intrapsychic images. Second, we consider the dreamwork practices of association, amplification, and animation and how these same methods may be and have been applied to working with our memory-images.

The second half of this book is dedicated to stories of those who have experienced imaginal remembering. In Chapter 5, Angeline's and Rasputin's respective stories of abuse and neglect suggest that by imaginally engaging with traumatic memories, fully and courageously witnessing the traumatized self, we may find healing and transformation. In Chapter 6, through the stories of Aria and Jennifer, we come to understand that in approaching our memories imaginally, we may better know ourselves for the here and now. Lilly's story of birth and Julia's story of death, shared in Chapter 7, intimate that memories may be access points for phenomena that stand at the margins of our human *beingness*. When we enter our memories imaginally, we may also touch something sacred, soulful, and deeply meaningful about our life experiences. Chapter 8, sharing Anne's and Francis's stories of letting go of those we have loved, suggests that our memories are access points to both the departed we have known and the self who was in relationship with them; in reaching those of our past as they exist in our own psyche, we seem to make peace with our past for the sake of our current and future selves.

To be sure, these themes of trauma, knowing the self, the soulful moments of birth and death, and letting go to free ourselves are simply labels, ways to compile and categorize the experiences. This set is notably limited; I would imagine there are as many themes of imaginal remembering as there are experiences. The collection is intended only as a way in, an introduction to the possibilities.

Second, though I have categorized and compiled the stories into themes, in each story, more than one theme emerges and may even correspond to a theme discussed in another chapter. In Chapter 5, in the story of Rasputin and his green-carpeted triangle chamber, there is an unmistakable understanding of the self who learned to live as the neglected child and now is learning to extend into the world as a healing man. In Julia's story (shared in Chapter 7) of meeting the memory-image of her father who has passed, she witnessed an aspect of her current life that desires healing, a relationship with her estranged brother that seems to beckon resurrection.

Third, these themes didn't emerge from ego intention, where the one who remembered set out to work with their memory as a way to make peace with themselves, for example. Rather, the memory seemed to choose itself, surfacing at just the right moment to be consciously invited by the rememberer to the imaginal remembering session. Through the rememberer's attentiveness to the memory-images, they seemed to open with animation and autonomy, as if to whisper the deepest longings of the soul.

Fourth, and finally, while the themes did seem to emerge, they are naturally biased by me as the researcher and even perhaps by the ego of the rememberer who had to state aloud what the intrapsychic images shared. We shall never know absolutely if these memory-images identified themselves with my articulated theme.

You may notice that the stories flow in a consistent pattern, both revealing the living images of memory as well as the process of imaginal remembering. In each case, I start with the memory the participants shared; then I recount their imaginal remembering experience. Along the way, I point out some of the symbols within the experience and suggest how they might deepen the wisdom offered and insight gleaned from the memory-images. Let me unpack this by way of an example. Returning to my childhood memory and the subsequent imaginal remembering experience I shared, the memory-image presented a ladybug that we might see as a symbol. The ladybug's association to life energy, rebirth, and awakenings of the deeper aspects of the psyche (coming when I needed encouragement to see this path of imaginal remembering forward) would be an analysis of that symbol.

The symbols emerging in imaginal remembering experiences that are shared in later chapters are considered both from an association (personal) and amplification (transpersonal) perspective. For example, as we will read in Chapter 6, Jennifer's sense of abandoning others may be personally associated to her own fear of abandonment. Yet with amplification, we might also see it is born of the archetypal urging, imaged in the Greek Goddess Artemis, to find within ourselves, and our natural world, strength and comfort. Of course, the animation, the way in which the images choose to present, is the best guide of all.

We approach the stories in this way:

- First, we listen to the memory because it shares with us important communications of the way in which the rememberer holds the memory and why it might be important for the psyche to now voice it.

- Second, the imaginal remembering experience is told as if it is happening right now, in present tense. We do this because to cradle the memory as if it is in the present is to invite our presence to it, including an attitude of openness. It relieves the fixedness that is anchored by the past and allows for the memory-image to shift and reshape based on its autonomy and wisdom. In this way, it urges the ego to accept that the memory-image functions of its own accord, not necessarily participating in the experience in the same way as the original event or at least how it's been recalled. This is critically important when our memory-images are of those whom we've known in the physical world. In imaginal remembering, we don't force these images to behave in the ways we've identified them based on our past or even current perspectives for we see them as psychic images, distinguishing them from the physical world.

- Third, in the analysis offered throughout, we approach the animate and autonomous images from association and amplification stances, turning toward the living images in a way that helps to reveal their communications with the self without pinning them down or fixating upon an ego-perspective of their meanings.

The ability to see our memories in this way, to invite our own self to reflect upon them differently than we have, may offer us something. Perhaps that offering is healing or creativity or empowerment; I suppose this all depends on the rememberer, the memory, and the living images of that memory. Ultimately, it is for you, the reader, to decide whether there is something to this notion of imaginal remembering. For my part, and based on my research, I see it as potentially a work of and for the soul.

PART I

THE WHY, WHAT, AND HOW OF
IMAGINAL REMEMBERING

And I enter the fields and roomy
chambers of memory, where are the
treasures of countless images,
imported into it from all manner of
things by the senses.
~ St. Augustine, *Confessions*

CHAPTER 2

MAKING THE CASE:
MEMORY AS IMAGINAL

Etymologically, *imagination* is derived from the 14th-century Middle English term *ymaginacion*, which roughly translates as the ability of the mind to form and manipulate images. Image is how psyche makes itself conscious. Our memories as

> Everything of which we are conscious is an image and . . . image is psyche.
> ~ C. G. Jung[3]

psychic phenomena are revealed as images when we're made consciously aware of them.

Given that *image* is the root of the term *imagination*, it's hardly a leap to connect image to imagination. Connecting memory to imagination is not so straightforward. In the first half of this chapter, I attempt to bridge the two by first connecting memory to image, specifically psychic image. In the second half of the chapter, I tender the argument that given memory is image, it's influenced by the imagination.

This chapter includes the fruits of my original research that began with just a hunch that our memories are psychic images and could be engaged imaginally. Sweet conversations with my daughter in which she imagistically held my hand and skipped me down her memory lane seeded that hunch, possibly because she and I remembered shared experiences quite differently. Yet the way in which she waxed poetic, with rich sensorial and emotional depictions, made me believe her versions as much, if not more, than I trusted in my own.

If you are the skeptic, this chapter is for you. After reading this you are likely to arrive at one of three positions. On one side, you may come to decide what's seemed preposterous is simply a reversal of how to look at this thing called memory, finding that what we see as our past may also be imaged as the present and possibly the future. On the other side, you may feel tested but that much more confident in seeing memory as immutable, objective, and precise. In either case, I will hold your opinion up with respect and know that you are not so dissimilar from me or many of those that I have engaged with along this path. It's not a simple or easy to task to call imaginative what have been the concrete pylons of our lived past. Those who find themselves in the third position, that fluid space that defies a binary this or that, I hope you journey on and allow yourself as much time as you need before you label yourself a skeptic or a believer.

What is Memory?

The subject of memory is fertile soil, having been worked-over countless times and as far back as ancient civilizations. Its sheer fecundity has reaped a multitude of theories and musings of both complementary and contradictory natures. Let me take you on a brief, chronological tour of some highlights.

Beginning with the ancient Greeks, Socrates described memory as imprint on a wax block, and Aristotle spoke of memory as image and memory's connection to soma, to the body.[4] The yogic sage Patañjali wrote of karma as a memory trace, a thought or action destined to repeat itself because it's been explicitly or implicitly recorded in the psyche of the individual who planted the karmic seed through his or her original thought or action.[5] Augustine, a Byzantine Empire theologian, praised his god for the blessing of remembering. The medieval theologian Thomas Aquinas questioned whether memory existed within the soul, answering that it's neither of the soul nor the intellect. During the Renaissance, humanists extolled the virtue of memory, and the empiricist John Locke, in the age of Enlightenment, provided a positivistic approach to memory retention. During the Romantic period, the philosophers Arthur Schopenhauer and Friedrich Nietzsche challenged a definition of memory as a rational, historical phenomenon; rather they argued it's influenced by psychological factors.

Physiologist Ewald Hering tied memory to the unconscious, and philosopher Henri Bergson argued that there are two forms of memory, one of which is actively imagined. The psychologist Sigmund Freud distrusted that all memories are historically factual. The memory researcher and biologist Richard Semon studied a biological storage (engram) of memory. The writer Rudolf Borchardt argued that the poet is a memory in a living, mercurial form. The renowned writer Marcel Proust used the role of involuntary memory as a central tenet for his monumental novel *In Search of Lost Time*. The philosopher Maurice Halbwachs conceptualized and wrote of collective memory. The psychologist C.G. Jung returned to his memories in later years as a source of self-reflection. The historian Pierre Nora argued that history and memory lie in opposition, the former static, and the latter animated.

The point of this whirlwind tour is to demonstrate that memory has inspired and bewildered, expanding into a wide range of theories that are still considered yet unproven (as we shall see) even today. There's still room, it seems, for tilling and tending the subject.

Memory in Modernity

Even scientific approaches among the modern fields of research psychology, neuroscience, biology, and physics complement and are complemented by an imaginal approach toward memory. Such an imaginal method seems to relieve memory of the cultural edict to see it as fixed and true rather than as a psychic phenomenon that shapes our psychologies specifically as we relate to our past, present, and future.

The research psychologist and Harvard professor Daniel Schacter explored decades of his own and others' research in *Searching for Memory*, writing, "We now know enough about . . . memories . . . to demolish another long-standing myth: that memories are passive or literal recordings of reality."[6] He then spent more than 300 pages articulating both psychological and neuroscientific research that demonstrates how we must abandon our desire to judge memories in a binary litmus test of true or false. The act of recalling a specific past event is influenced by the present self. This notion of true or false memory is an important one for several scholars, especially in the context of recovering repressed and false memories. I welcome it as helping to dislodge the perspective that memory is the fixed preservation of a previous physical realm experience. To be clear, this book neither looks to authenticate nor falsify memories nor attempts to suggest imaginal remembering is a means by which we can recover memory. Rather, the practice of imaginal remembering seeks to work with memory-images as psychic phenomena in a way that has the potential to impact our relationships to ourselves, others, and our past, present, and future. This begins by attempting to dismantle the cultural belief that our memories are static and precise.

In part, Daniel Schacter supported his challenge to the theory of engrams, the physical traces of memories existing in the brain, by sharing that brain imaging does not prove that brain activity is associated to the retrieval of a stored memory trace. Rather, such activity may be the search for cues that prompt remembering. These cues are an important part of memory retrieval where the more richly encoded the event, the more material from which to elicit or trigger a recollection. Our current ability to access cues that retrieve memories is both influenced by the actual experience as well as our current state (where a currently experienced phenomenon may provoke a memory cue).

For example, on a trip to Philadelphia, I had arrived at my hotel late one evening. When I entered the lobby to check-in, I noticed a subtle but perceptible scent, hints of herb and iris comingled with sandalwood and musk. I stood for a moment in the lobby, but rather than pay attention to its modern décor of red and grey tapestry lit up by cylindrical, frosted chandeliers, in my mind's eye, I saw a sunlit lobby that looked out on a bustling sidewalk. Teak furniture and tropical plants were situated against the windowed walls. All but the scent was different. I recalled then staying at this hotel chain in San Francisco, their signature scent being a strong cue that pulled me back several years before to a location on the opposite side of the country.

Returning to the idea that our memories are not engrams, Schacter reasoned that memory loss is not always associated to brain damage nor is brain damage essential to memory loss, providing another neuroscientific argument against the notion of physical traces of memory. Rather than to access one precise region of the brain, the act of remembering constellates several areas, the retrieved memory being "a construction with many contributors."[7] To this end, Schacter argued that the brain, unlike a computer that retrieves information, is an organ for remembering experiences, where the activity of remembering is influenced by the present psychology of the one who remembers. This idea that the brain facilitates remembering rather than stores memory supports the notion of memory-images as animate, autonomous psychic images for it offers a plausible neuroscientific argument: instead of functioning as the storage depot for memories as fixed information, the brain is engaged in the activity of remembering.

The Multiple Meanings of Memory

I have been using the term *memory* as if it is just one thing, one specific phenomenon, but there are different types of memory— though we don't necessarily think of memory as coming in types. Yet the notion is intuitive when those types are explained, and the topic is important here because imaginal remembering appears most well-suited for one particular type of memory. The generally accepted break down and associated terminology of the primary types of memory are: *semantic, procedural,* and *episodic.* There are also secondary types that can be strongly aligned with one of these primary types, two being *autobiographical memory* and *explicit/implicit memory.* These two are particularly important when considering the notion of imaginal remembering, but since they further dimensionalize a primary type of memory, we shall begin with these three.

Semantic memory is what we might think of as knowledge. It is knowing that my name is Daphne and that I have two children. It is also knowing where the keys to my car are supposed to hang (if I don't forget to place them there when I return home). *Procedural memory* is the kind of memory that allows us to, still groggy, remember how to run the coffee maker or to, seemingly without any attention paid to the matter, tie our shoes. Finally, there is *episodic memory*. This is the memory that is connected to past events; aptly named, it is the memory of specific episodes and incidents. It is the memory of the birth of a child, the death of a loved one, or even the walk we took two weeks ago when we were unexpectedly caught outside in the cold rain.

Our attention in this book is focused on episodic memory for these are the memories of deep relevance for us in how they shape the self. This is a rather important distinction because, though extensive research has been undertaken by biologists and neuroscientists to study the brain's role in memory, much of that work was related to *learning memory* (aligned with procedural and semantic memory) and was primarily conducted among some of the simplest forms of sea creatures.[8,9]

Yet, it's difficult to partition these types of memory entirely, where there is obvious overlap in how we might think of them. Daniel Schacter helped to communicate the difference between semantic and episodic memory—knowing and remembering—through the case study of Gene, a man who suffered a severe head injury in a motorcycle accident.[10] Gene could recall semantic memories, knowing that he had owned motorcycles and a summer cottage, for instance. However, Gene, having no episodic memory, could not recall experiences of his life. He had no memories, for example, of riding those motorcycles. As Gene's case demonstrates, both semantic and episodic memories can be autobiographical in nature, meaning both types of memory can relate to our personal lives.

The same can be thought of with procedural memory. Schacter didn't share whether Gene was still able to ride those motorcycles, meaning whether the mind-body connection of how to sit and lean, and increase and decrease the speed of the vehicle, was still quite available to him after the accident. However, often when we're in those moments of moving our bodies in a way that is very familiar to us (perhaps through riding a motorcycle, or playing a piano, or dancing) we can identify ourselves with this movement. I will speak to this later and throughout this book—the somatic aspects of our memory. For now, let me suggest that episodic memory which is autobiographical (of our own personal life experiences) is highly germane to imaginal remembering, but the relevance of the other two, semantic and procedural, should not be dismissed in imaginal remembering because of the impact they have on our bodies, our somatic psychology. As we shall see with Rasputin in Chapter 5, the intimate semantic details of the green carpeting and wooden, doweled back of the piano, moved him deeply into the imaginal remembering experience. In Chapter 7, Lilly's procedural memory of turning the knob of a door, when purposefully slowed down so that she could fully experience her imaginal hand on the imaginal handle, became the entry way into a most sacred memory-image.

Why then is episodic memory primarily identified with shaping who we are? To help answer this, it's helpful to consider the idea of *autonoetic consciousness*. The research psychologists Mark Wheeler, Donald Stuss, and Endel Tulving referred to episodic memory as "mental time travel"—the notion that an individual can, through memory, return to a previous point in life as if traveling back to another time.[11] The ability to do this, they argued, is due to autonoetic consciousness that allows the individual to simultaneously recall a past event and be aware that she is doing just that—experiencing a recollection. Autonoetic means self-reflection, an ability to acknowledge the existence of one's individual self and experiences of that self. In other words, by remembering an episodic memory, we're aware of our self as engaging in the experience of remembering. This is an important point for imaginal remembering, for in doing so, we're not just recalling a memory. Rather, we are engaging with it, witnessing the self as it engages with other aspects of that same self which manifest as intrapsychic images.

Only the episodic (not semantic nor procedural) type of memory is true memory, according to professor of psychological and brain sciences, Stan Klein, for it's the only one among the three that holds the past as its frame of reference, meaning that it does not categorically bring into consciousness events of the past explicitly to navigate one's current or future position. It recalls a past event for the sake of the past. In making this argument, Klein stressed that simply to retrieve content of the past (for example, to know my name is Daphne or to tie my shoe as I learned years go) does not mean that I am remembering. Rather, to be considered an experience of remembering (as opposed to knowing, believing, or imagining), "the retrieved content must be connected to a pre-reflective mode of awareness—autonoesis—in which the occurrent experience evokes a feeling of reliving one's past."[12]

Thus, for Klein, the brain's functions of encoding, storage, and retrieval are important aspects in the production of memory, but they're not the memory itself for a memory requires autonoesis, that self-reflective capacity. In other words, Klein, as a scholar of brain sciences, clarified that the brain's functions of encoding, storage, and retrieval enable our ability to remember; however, *memories are not epiphenomena of brain activity; rather they are phenomenological experiences.* A memory, then, is a memory only insofar as the self experiences it as such, aware of itself reflecting upon itself. This is important to the idea of imaginal remembering for it: (1) supports a shift from seeing memories as fixed and accurate presentations of past events to experiencing them as psychic phenomena which are influenced by the self who reflects upon them; and (2) encourages an approach to memory that is phenomenological and self-reflective, ideas we shall pursue further in Chapter 4.

This notion of a memory requiring self-reflection conflicts with another distinction of memory: *explicit* and *implicit.* Simply, *explicit memory* is a term used to describe memory that's held in conscious awareness, whereas *implicit memory* is the term for memory that is unconscious, guiding our behaviors and perceptions seemingly without our conscious awareness.

Let me unpack this idea of explicit versus implicit memory by way of an example. I know a teacher who is quite aware that she's inclined to present feedback to her students as "constructive criticism," versus praise, rationalizing that she was taught in the same manner so that she, and thus her students, would rise to higher standards. Yet, she's unaware that when she delivers such constructive criticism, she generally does so by using a shrill, booming voice, and staring with disdain as she shakes her head and wags her finger at her students (where the "constructive" aspect is often lost to the overwhelmingly critical tone). I once pointed out to her the way in which she delivers her critiques. She was stunned and remorseful of her unconscious behaviors. She then recalled to me that her distant and often cruel mother took the same the approach with her when she was a child.

That she is inclined toward "constructive criticism" because this was her teacher's method, this is *explicit*—she's consciously aware and purposefully driven to provide the type of feedback that was modeled by her teacher. However, the way in which she behaves (her delivery style as was modeled by her mother), that would be *implicit* because she has no conscious awareness that she's treating her students in this manner. I should point out that her delivery method (the parroted behavior of her mother) has not fully changed despite that when I pointed it out, what was implicit became explicit *in that moment*. Let me restate this, succinctly, as a segue to the next paragraph: she is conscious (explicit) of modeling her teacher's *type* of feedback; in contrast, she is unconscious (implicit) of modeling her mother's *style* of criticism.

So here's where it gets tricky. Stan Klein argued that there is no implicit or unconscious memory because, by his definition, memory is only memory as it's a past event raised into conscious awareness and reflected upon as such.[13] In other words, memory can *only* be explicit, because the process of remembering requires conscious self-reflection. The psychologist Martin Conway, though, reasoned that implicit memories or the unconscious content of past events may unknowingly have an enduring effect on our conscious attitudes and behaviors.[14]

Let's return to the teacher I spoke of above. In Klein's model of memory, there is no implicit memory of her mother treating her in this way. Rather, her behavior is rooted in the implicit residual content of past events (as Conway's model suggests). Once I called her attention to her physical behaviors (raising her voice, shaking her head, and wagging her finger), she remembered her mother behaving in the same manner. The content of the past became explicit to her *in the moment* that I described her behaviors to her. However, that content continues to slip its way back into the unconscious (perhaps because it is painful and thus avoided), becoming implicit content that continues to, without conscious awareness, shape her behaviors.

Because I believe both Klein and Conway make compelling arguments, I prefer to not label *memory itself* as implicit or explicit. Rather, I suggest we assign these descriptors to *the contents* of our psyches that might inform our attitudes and behaviors. Returning to the teacher example: in this case, we would label her mother's and her teacher's behaviors as the contents of her past that influence her current behaviors. The contents of her mother's behavior (when not brought into conscious awareness) are implicit (she is unconscious of

their influence on her own behavior); the contents of her teacher's
behaviors are explicit (because she holds them in awareness,
consciously employing the content to shape her own behaviors).

Such distinctions of implicit and explicit residual content surfaced
in research among brain damaged individuals who were still
influenced by past experiences even though they could no longer
recall those experiences.[15] Further, research among infants suggests
that structures of the brain supporting implicit residual content are
developed prior to the existences of structures that support explicit
content. The implications of these studies are fascinating. That
implicit content of past events exists before and perhaps even after
explicit content is gone speaks to the mystery and influence of the
content of our memories especially in developing and supporting our
sense of self. It helps ease the resistance to approaching our
memories imaginally because it invites us to embrace their perplexing
nature.

The Self and Memory

The notion of memory as paramount to the self is critical to the
subject of imaginal remembering because it helps to explain why the
malleability of our memories turns out to be quite necessary for the
health of our psyches, a premise from which imaginal remembering is
based. This is a foundational concept in the study of *autobiographical
memory*, a type of memory that researchers specifically and
systematically studied after identifying episodic, semantic, and
procedural memory.[16,17] Autobiographical memory speaks to those
memories that relate directly to oneself; thus, it is influenced by a
great many things to include the facts of our lives (semantic) as well
as the specific sensorial, perceptual elements of the events of our
lives (episodic). Our autobiographical memories are fundamentally
significant to the way in which we see ourselves and experience the
world, even helping to explain why we might see and experience
ourselves and our memories differently across stages of our lives.

Martin Conway and Christopher Pleydell-Pearce suggested that
our autobiographical memories are transitory and/or dynamic in
nature because they are highly influenced by what the authors refer to
as the *working self*.[18] This working self is that aspect of the self that

functions in the here and now to set goals and reinforce those goals with supportive images that are drawn from the individual's *autobiographical knowledge base*. This base is populated with knowledge related to one's lived experiences, and the contents are described by the specificity of information regarding that lived experience. For instance, the contents could be anything from a lifetime period (for a time I lived as a child in Texas) to general events (as a little girl, we drove many hours to visit my grandmother in Missouri), to quite specific bits of data rich with vivid, sensorial details (when we arrived at her home, we were greeted by the scent of a beef stew simmering in a worn stock pot on the stove; she used red onions in that soup, cut in circles, and I can recall opening the lid of the pot and watching the little onion rings swirling atop the broth).

According to Conway, the working self then operates in congruence with the autobiographical knowledge base in what Conway referred to as the Self-Memory-System (SMS), striving toward setting and reinforcing the goals set by the working self. Unpacking this with an example: my working self identifies with the goal of being a strong, independent woman; thus, the memories I draw upon of my grandmother (who, in part, raised me) support my working self. I remember that pot of

> It seems then that autobiographical memory is dominated by the 'force' or 'demand' of coherence. . . . A coherent self will have high self-esteem and a strong positive sense of well-being.
> ~ Martin Conway[19]

stew was left for us because she, as a single woman who had raised three daughters on her own, worked the night shift as a psychiatric nurse so that she could also work another day job and make ends meet. I recall listening to her stories of how she put herself through nursing school and her two brothers through engineering school in the 1930s.

My memories of her feed my own goal to be a strong, independent woman because I look back and see that she role-modeled this for me at important developmental stages of my life. As this example demonstrates, the working self monitors its relationship to the autobiographical knowledge base, selecting and deselecting bits of factual data so that specific life experiences are recalled in order to support the self's perspective of itself. Conway described this congruence as *self-coherence*, a function that is involved with encoding, remembering, and re-encoding these bits of factual data in a way that shapes the memory and our access to the contents of that memory.

In the example of my working self identifying as a strong, independent woman, I may easily recall times in which I have stood strong in the face of difficulty because such recollections reinforce my goal to be a strong, independent woman. As it happens, coherence may be at odds with "correspondence" (the notion that lived experience should directly correspond to memory) for at least two reasons. First, the sheer amount of historical data of lived experiences would likely be overwhelming. Second, not all our memories support the way in which the self perceives itself (e.g. I may easily forget the times I leaned on my husband, Dan, to face the challenges of our shared life because to recall such events might challenge my working self's goal). For healthy individuals, coherence between our memories and our perspective of ourselves is necessary for the self to function effectively. Memories ideally would support our self-identity and the goals we have set out to achieve. These ideas are important for imaginal remembering if for no other reason that they continue to chip away at our culture's paradigm of seeing memories as fixed and precise.

The Brains Behind Self and Memory

If imaginal remembering allows us to explore our deepest sense of the self, as I've seen time and time again, then we must continue to ask what is the self, and then, what role does memory play in the making and maintaining of the self? In 2010, the neuroscientist Antonio Damasio took up this question in the book, *Self Comes to Mind: Constructing the Conscious Brain*. Damasio wrote as a materialist, explicitly crediting brain matter with unproven (at least as of the time of this

> The title of this book, as well as its first pages, leave no doubt that in approaching the conscious mind, I privilege the self.
> ~Antonio Damasio[20]

writing) hypotheses despite his copious and thorough citations of research. Yet he cogently offered an argument of how the brain is *involved* in development of consciousness that affords an understanding or an awareness of the personal self that, in full loop, develops consciousness. Regardless of whether the brain leads or follows (an unknown guidance), according to Damasio, the brain is involved in consciousness by way of map-making and image-making. Further, memory is paramount to consciousness which is inextricably intertwined with the self.

For Damasio, self is not an entity of the individual but the way in which the individual's brain processes. He spoke of the self as both an observer and as a knower, taking in information as well as reflecting upon such information including that which is drawn from our lived experiences. Whether entity or process, Damasio described the self as something in the making and highly influenced by experiences and the reflection upon those experiences— memory. In fact, Damasio seated the conversation of memory directly in the realm of consciousness and self. He argued that memory is

> The ultimate consequences of consciousness come by way of memory . . . . Memory is responsible for ceaselessly placing the self in an evanescent here and now between a thoroughly lived past and an anticipated future.
> ~ Antonio Damasio[21]

responsible for allowing an individual to hold the perspectives of imagining one's own well-being as well as the well-being of one's society. To this end, he credited memory with the fundamental biological value of survival (basic homeostasis) that yields, at a higher level, to a sense of individual and social well-being (sociocultural homeostasis).

What does it mean to place memory, via self, via consciousness, in the realm of the brain? For Damasio, it means an orchestration of several areas of the brain that work in seamless harmony. He argued that the brain makes maps, informing itself along the way. By making these maps, the brain creates images that function as transient maps of all things both within and beyond us. The brain even makes maps of the brain's making of maps, reflecting upon its self-reflection, so to speak. We see then that maps are images and images are maps, in a never-ending loop of the brain speaking to itself about itself and about its relationship to other as object.

Keeping in mind that Damasio described the self as a process rather than an entity, a self becoming rather than a self that is, he argued that these images are exhibited to consciousness in a way that supports development of the autobiographical self, that aspect of the self that acknowledges the world, is influenced by the world, and in turn acknowledges the influence of the world with which it engages. This notion of image-selection is strikingly similar to the findings of Martin Conway, et al., as described earlier. However, for Damasio, this selection is biologically driven. Why does this matter to imaginal remembering? Because it supports the notion that our memories are images not unlike our dreams; thus, they might be approached in a similar way. It is intriguing to think that even the hard sciences might somehow be persuaded to find support for such an idea. Let's continue to explore just how that may be the case.

This orchestration of map-making and image-making occur in two material spaces of the brain, what Demasio calls the *dispositional space* and the *image space*. The dispositional space is both the warehouse of our knowledge and the blueprints to reconstruct that knowledge; it's responsible for generating the images but not for displaying them to consciousness—that's the work of the image space. The dispositional space then holds implicit or unconscious content while the image space is the exhibition hall, making that content explicit to consciousness. However, even the images that remain unconscious are still highly influential in developing the self, as we've discussed earlier in this chapter in our conversation regarding implicit and explicit content of memories. In fact, Damasio argued that it may be in the unconscious space where images most significantly influence the autobiographical self—specifically by way of maturing the self gradually, reshaping one's memories over time and multiple life experiences in ways that cultivate the self but also rework memories to support that cultivation.

Damasio described this intricate and elaborate map- and image-making, selecting, and exhibiting process as what happens for both memory and imagination. Regarding memory, Damasio argued that because it creates maps, the brain need not store each memory, each object (to include experiences) with which it has come into contact, as an *engram*. Rather the map is like a dexterous formula that tells the brain how to reconstruct the image. In other words, the image of an episodic, autobiographical memory is not a perfect representation of the lived experience; it is a remembrance (as in a re-creation, using the brain's current perceptual material) of what occurred. Here, of course, we have a neuroscientific perspective as to why memory should never be regarded as static—if memory is always and already a re-creation, this opens the door to the further acts of creation that occur in imaginal remembering.

In terms of the imagination, Damasio saw this same process of reconstruction involved in the process of imagination, where the brain recalls and then manipulates images, as if to suit its fancy. He saw imagination as the greatest benefit of consciousness because it allows the individual to navigate the unknown waters of the future by way of intersecting memory with imagination. In Julia's story that you'll read about in Chapter 7, you'll see how the memory of her father's passing, and the subsequent recollections this memory ushered into consciousness, invited Julia to imagine a way of being in relationship with her estranged brother. Her imagination, which was supported by her memories, engaged her conscious self in an imaginal dialogue with her brother. In this encounter, Julia witnessed not only her own deeply buried emotions but possibly those of her brother, emotions she had otherwise consciously resisted. Through excavating what was buried, Julia imagined, imaginally witnessed, a way in which she might approach a future, physical encounter with her brother. You see then, imagination requires memory that in turn requires psychic images that are also required by imagination. Tightly woven are memory, image, imagination, and self from neuroscientific and imaginal remembering perspectives.

Memory as Morphic Fields

Now that we have considered some mainstream support for seeing our memories as images and approaching them imaginally, let's have a go at an altogether different reason why we might do well to take a preposterous perspective of memory. The biologist Rupert Sheldrake offered salient challenges to the theory of memory traces. Rather than function as a storage depot of engrams, argued Sheldrake, the brain, or more broadly speaking the nervous system, allows for engagement with morphic fields. *Morphic field* is Sheldrake's term for a hypothesized "field within and around a morphic unit" that "organizes [the] characteristic structure and pattern of activity" of that morphic unit.[22]

A morphic unit may be anything from an atom to a human to a galaxy. The morphic unit, a chimpanzee, for example, is influenced by the morphic field through what Sheldrake called morphic resonance. Through this influence, the chimpanzee can know, engage, function, and react to stimuli (including environments) of which this particular chimp has never had direct experience. In other words, habituation (diminished response to stimuli) and sensitization (enhanced response to stimuli) learning, as described by the neuropsychiatrist Eric Kandel,[23] are already known by the chimpanzee even though it never directly experienced stimuli that would create such learning. Rather, this chimp benefits from the learning of chimpanzees whose experiences predate his own. In other words, learning memory is not necessarily acquired through direct experience.

Rupert Sheldrake offered many examples that support his hypothesis of morphic fields,[24] examples that will help us to better understand and accept the fruits of imaginal remembering which we'll get to momentarily. First, some examples. One regards a series of experiments lasting more than 30 years in which Harvard researchers trained rats to find their way through a water maze. In the beginning, the first cohort of rats averaged 165 errors in their attempts to escape. This had lowered to an average of 20 errors by the time the thirtieth generation was trialed. To control for rat intelligence, the lead investigator chose the least intelligent rats of that generation. Because the results were so difficult to accept, researchers in Scotland and Australia replicated the study and found that even their first-generation rats had far fewer errors than were seen among the initial Harvard cohort. Likewise, in the Scottish and Australian research, the rates of learning progressively increased in the generations that followed.

From these studies, they concluded that the water maze learning could not simply be explained as matter of inheritance. Sheldrake argued it was proof of morphic resonance and morphic fields. So why does this matter to imaginal remembering? Because the rats, in this case, were tapping into something belonging not to their own direct experiences. Rather, this morphic field, as Sheldrake called it, seems to be a collective field, a web, so to speak, to which we all have access. Hold this thought for a moment.

The notion of a morphic field is like the physicist David Bohm's perspective of the implicate order (the unity of all), an idea based on quantum theory. Bohm saw the universe as a holomovement that holds the implicate order.[25] Analogous to a hologram, within the holomovement, each aspect holds information about the entire object. Therefore, each individual part of the universe that unfolds in the explicate order (what we observe and experience in the physical world) is enfolded in the implicate order. As way of example, Bohm asked his reader to imagine ink droplets (representing the unfolded) enfolded, through mechanical stirring, into a fluid until their individual particles become undetectable. If the stirring is reversed, the ink droplets return, unfolded in the fluid. Bohm argued that this movement of enfolding and unfolding is universal.[26] The unfolded, that we experience as stable and autonomous patterns, are maintained by the continual, inherent process of enfoldment and unfoldment. Thus, an experience is an unfolded, explicate order phenomenon that then is enfolded back into the implicate order. Bohm suggested that the processes of enfoldment and unfoldment could, repeated often enough, develop what Sheldrake referred to as morphic fields.

From this, we might hypothesize that a memory is an explicate order phenomenon experienced through morphic resonance. A specific contribution that Sheldrake's and Bohm's theories offer to the hypothesis that memories are autonomous and animated psychic images is their suggestions that memories are, perhaps, something other than the phenomenon of recalling an individual experience. In other words, memory may be something more or entirely separate from how it is currently perceived—as the psychic replaying of a past event. Conceivably, memories may be the phenomenon of engaging something other than remnants of our previously experienced physical world. As you will see in the chapters of Part II, many of the images that arise during imaginal remembering relate to something directly inexplicable to the rememberer.

You may recall from Chapter 1 the idea of approaching our dream and our imaginal remembering phenomena from an amplification perspective, drawing upon the artifacts of ancient cultures and cultures other than our own to help us understand the deeper meanings of the symbols that surface in these phenomena. The symbols seem to arise from something other than the physical remnants of the rememberer's or dreamer's past lived experiences because the self has no conscious understanding of, no personal association to, them. C.G. Jung called this something other the *collective unconscious*. Might not the collective unconscious be an aspect of the morphic field? If we think of it in this way, we are better able to understand, for example, why Lilly, in Chapter 7, imaginally witnessed her grandmother's spirit as a cloud that morphs into a bird. As ancient texts and artifacts tell us, these images, the cloud and the bird, may be manifestations of the divine, spiritualization, and the soul, important themes in Lilly's sacred story of birth and death. In Chapter 8, Francis's imaginal remembering experience, about saying goodbye to her mother, revealed a mirror that is possibly a symbol of the soul and a passing from one world onto another.

Before bridging the next half of the chasm, linking memory to imagination, I want to recap where we have been in connecting memory to image.

- First, memory is critical to the development of the self and consciousness specifically as memory-images.

- Second, memory can be seen as fluid, malleable, adaptive, and influenced by the past, the present, and the imagined future—in other words, memory is constructed and reconstructed.

- Third, the brain is not necessarily the storage depot for memory; rather this fantastic part of our physical being enables access to our memories by agency of image- and map-making.

- Fourth, memory is not necessarily accessing memory traces of physically experienced phenomena; indeed, memory might be the way in which we engage with the nonphysical world, namely the collective unconscious and morphic fields.

With that, we begin to explore the intricate interweaving of memory and imagination. With each step, we move nearer to approaching our memories imaginatively, coming to imaginally remember our past for the sake of our present and future.

Memory as Image and of the Imagination

Aristotle argued that "memory, even the memory of concepts, cannot exist apart from imagery," for the "psychic faculty [of] memory belongs . . . to that which imagination must be assigned."[27] This ancient Greek philosopher, so foundational to our current empirical, Western culture, posited the imaginative-orientation of memory.

The Sufi scholar Henri Corbin invited us to imagine our memories as new beginnings, arguing that if we saw our memories as nothing but the remains of what is over and done, we would not return to them again and again. Rather, we sift through these remnants of our past as if to finish what still feels wanting, and by doing so, "we are in fact consummating our own future."[29] Here again we might think of Julia, in Chapter 7, who by spending time in the memory-image of her father's passing, offered a way into a future relationship with her brother. Or we might think of Angeline, in Chapter 5, who by engaging with the traumatic memory of escaping an abusive relationship has been able to find healing and preemptively address potential future challenges of her current relationship. Corbin's invitation to see memory in a futuristic sense is particularly welcoming in an argument for approaching memory imaginatively.

> If the past were really what we believe it to be, that is, completed and closed, it would not be the grounds of such vehement discussions.
> ~ Henri Corbin[28]

The Constructed Memory

Despite having initially given memory a great deal of thought and attention, Sigmund Freud appeared to abandon the subject in the early 1900s because, it seemed, memory had lost his trust. In "Screen Memories," Freud argued that at least some memories are historically incorrect, woven from childhood phenomena and manipulated images from later-life-events that are "screened off" or repressed into the unconscious. These *screen memories* aren't precise images of past encounters. Rather they are the threads of historical events entwined with related, but repressed, lived experience content such that the final tapestry as a recollection is quite different than the historical phenomena to which it's been associated.

Freud perceived that memories, specifically memories of childhood, are images influenced by current physical and psychological circumstances. In some cases, such screen memories are psychologically mediated stand-ins for that which has been repressed. In other cases, the screen memories support currently held perspectives of the individual self by projecting backward fantasies that are perceived as memories to align the perceived

> A 'screen memory' [is] one which owes its value as a memory not to its own content but to the relation existing between that content and some other, that has been suppressed.
> ~ Sigmund Freud[30]

experiences of the past self with the self-identity of current self. This seems like modern psychologists' perspectives, spoken to in the first half of this chapter, of the working self that, in support of its goals, selects and deselects bits of data from our lived experiences to raise into conscious awareness. The individual remembers a past that supports his present circumstances, in the same vein as the contemporary research psychologist Martin Conway has found.

In part, Sigmund Freud's argument is centered on the vantage point of our memories: that of the third person observer. Those memories we view as the detached observer are naturally identified as altered versions of the historical event because we are viewing them as an observer, someone watching the event unfold, versus from a field perspective, the perspective of one engaged in, *in the field of*, the event. Freud claimed that this observer perspective demonstrates that the memory is not of the actual event but is of our memory of the event as it is pulled through the current self, twisted into a contemporary phenomenon that is perceived as aligned with an earlier experience. The phenomenon as the memory-image is both a remembering and an imagining—beginning with matter of the physical world, it is then reshaped, re-membered, by the imagination.

How do we reconcile the concern that all memories may then be judged as mere fabrications? Perhaps it is by agreeing to see them as neither true nor false. Daniel Schacter wrote extensively of this divisive subject. In the end, he contended that there must be some reconciliation between what's deemed as historical truth and narrative truth, where the former describes an actual

> We need to recognize that memories do not exist in one of two states—either true or false—and that the important task is to examine how and in what ways memory corresponds to reality.
> ~ Daniel Schacter[31]

event and the latter is the story an individual believes to be true because it is the way she remembers it having occurred. Relieving memory from the confines of being judged either true or false is critical to opening oneself to the experiences of imaginal remembering. Engaging with a memory-image as animate and autonomous requires a willingness to accept the image as neither historically accurate nor inaccurate but as "real" in terms of being psychic phenomenon that contributes to the shaping and reshaping of our personal psychologies. There is courage required to approach our memories in such an imaginative way, as we shall see.

The Temporally Exogenous Qualities of Memory

To set the stage for an imaginative consideration of memory, the philosopher Edward Casey began by comparing the discussions of the philosophers Thomas Hobbes and David Hume.[32] According to Casey, Hobbes considered memory and imagination as one and the same, for they both emerged from the senses. Hume, on the other hand, argued that the subtle differences between the two are related to each one's level of liveliness and animation, where memory has more life than does imagination. Casey challenged Hobbes and expanded upon the works of Hume.

First, he argued that memory is rooted in perception, whereas imagination isn't held to such an obligation. Second, Casey argued that whereas memory is connected to the past, imagination is free from such a bind. Third, memory is, according to Casey,

characterized by an ability to perceive a phenomenon as having
already occurred, where the products of the imagination are retained
only after they exist as an imaginative experience. Fourth, Casey
argued that familiarity is critical to memory but not necessary for
imagination. Fifth, Casey saw that memory differs from imagination
in the quality of one's beliefs towards them—we believe that a
memory has been, while we accept the musings of our imagination as
having no temporal or physical existence. As I see it, the distinctions
between memory and imagination as outlined by Casey have little to
do with their phenomenological differences but everything to do with
how they're perceived. In other words, as a culture, we judge memory
as something different than imagination. But is this judgment
warranted?

Not according to philosopher Gilbert Durand, who argued on
behalf of the imagination and memory as being more than what the
Cartesian culture affords them.[33] Durand held both phenomena in
such high regard that he associated them to the works of the soul,
speaking of both dream and memory phenomena as *active images*.
Durand credited these active images as having no exogenous, no
externally derived, limitations; this included their ability to transcend
time, blending past, present, and future. Memory-images as active
images are free, then, from temporal fixedness and other arbitrary
cultural confines.

Even Edward Casey, who carefully outlined the differences
between memory and imagination, did not suggest them to be
fundamentally separate.[34] Rather, he argued that memory and
imagination are conjoined in that as much as memory looks to the
past as a way to ground itself in perception, to that sensory act that
affords belief in an experience, it also looks toward imagination in the
way it presentifies not what *is* physically real but what appears *as*
physically real. In other words, though memory has roots in the
physical realm experience, it naturally presents itself as a psychic
experience, specifically as the memory-image.

Image and matter are cleaved through memory, where memory
reflectively images the matter of what was experienced in the past.
Henri Bergson spoke of *recollective memory* which is highly imagistic and
comingles our physical world experiences with our dream world
phenomena.[35] Recollective memory, or what we might think of as
episodic, autobiographical memory, lives at the crossroads between

matter and imagination. Memory-images, then, are the manifestation of imagined matter; they are agents of both the past and the imagination.

If we agree to free them from the empirical perspective that they are somehow fixed and static, we come to see that memories, through engagement with memory-images, "not only *represent* the past and matter; they actively *imagine* both."[36] Thus, memory-images not only re-present our past, but they shape and are reshaped by the present and the future. This then fits with Gilbert Durand's posit that memory is not a restoration of past experiences but is creative by nature—indeed, memory creates the self. Once again, the thesis resounds: memory is not passive, a concrete trace of a bygone event; rather it is the agent and the effect of the self who reflects upon it.

Let us then recognize that from depth psychologist to neuroscientist, cognitive researcher to philosopher, Ancient Greece to present day, scholars have subscribed to and argued for the notion that memories are psychic images shaped and reshaped by our self. The imagination is both responsible for the shaping and reshaping of memory, and likewise, is, itself, formed and informed by memory. Unconscious images, formed by past experiences (including those that manifest as dream images), may be highly influential to the development of the self, specifically the autobiographical self. Now we turn to a way in which we might approach memories as these psychic images that may have much to offer us given the chance.

CHAPTER 3

THE SOUL, SPIRIT, AND VIBRANCY OF LIVING IMAGES

How do you take a well-worn word and ask it to be something different, something more than what most cultures expect of it? That's the task when arguing the notion of a *living image*. In this chapter, you will find the ways in which I am trying to describe this aspect of living, this way of being. I lean on the writings of psychologists and philosophers to make the case that at least some intrapsychic phenomena are living in that they're animate and autonomous, moving outside of the ego's control. In the end, you will decide if this term is expansive enough to belong to what is neither fleshy nor breathing but nonetheless brings us deeper to soul, closer to spirit, and makes our lives even more vibrant because of our courage to engage with it.

James Hillman, the author and depth psychologist, wrote, "Our psychic substance consists of images; our being is imaginal being, an existence in imagination. We are indeed such stuff as dreams are made of."[37] Hillman then tied the imaginal to the soul, arguing that psychology, as the work of and for the soul, is best achieved through engagement with the imaginal, with the image. In this way, Hillman described image not as an object but as an encounter, specifically an experience with the psyche and for the soul. *Living image*, then, is set free from the construct that it exists as an entity; rather, we come to appreciate it as an experience.

I believe I first heard of the term *living image* when I was introduced to the work of the psychologist and Pacifica Graduate Institute founder Stephen Aizenstat.[38,39] He was describing dream images, using the term living image without precisely defining what living meant. Perhaps this lack of definition was making the point that living, in terms of living images, is a sensibility rather than a definable metric—*a way of being* rather than a *being*. James Hillman's writings also posit that psychic images, when met as living images, may be realized as *psychopomps*.[40,41] The term psychopomp is derived from the Greek word *psuchopompos*,

> When an image is realized—fully imagined as a living being other than myself—then it becomes a psychopompos, a guide with a soul having its own inherent limitation and necessity.
> ~ James Hillman[42]

which translates to guide of souls. The ancient Greeks, along with many other cultures and religions, believed that these spiritual beings (depicted in many ways including angels, the Grim Reaper, and animals) ushered the soul from its Earthly presence to the afterlife. Some cultures see shamans as performing the role of the psychopomp.

Depth psychology also suspects that dream figures play this role, where a wise man or woman in a dream might be the guide who is inviting the dreamer's soul towards something else, something other. Thus, the psychopomp may not only guide the soul at the point of literal death but also in moments of symbolic death and rebirth. In some ways, Aria's story in Chapter 6 intimates such a notion, where the image of her younger self, whom Aria meets again in the space of a long-ago kitchen, is ushering Aria through a death/rebirth process and into a new way of being.

Indeed, C.G. Jung turned toward these psychic images to move through a troubling time in his adult life. Jung's *nekyia* (a term used to describe Jung's perusal of the unconscious) was the way in which, Jung came to, in the words of James Hillman, "Know Thyself."[43] But this "thyself" wasn't just one person; it was the plurality of images that make up the psyche. To Know Thyself, then, is not a work of introspection that is held sway by the feelings, thoughts, and recollections of ego-consciousness. Rather, to Know Thyself is to suspend the authority of the ego and to turn to the imagination, where to Know Thyself inherently means to respect that Thyself is not "myself" for I am more than my own current lifespan, my own history. I am plurality by way of sharing in the collective unconscious, that primordial, autonomous part of the psyche that is like a limitless universal reservoir of all ancestral experiences. Perhaps we might think of its existence as the inherited aspects of the dispositional space to which Antonio Damasio referred,[44] or the morphic resonance as posited by Rupert Sheldrake.[45]

By paying heed to the images of the psyche, I am present to the images of the archetypes. Archetypes, often manifest as archetypal images, are what C.G. Jung referred to as "residues of ancestral life" made available to us through the collective or transpersonal unconscious.[46] You may recall the example I shared in Chapter 1 and will further explore in Chapter 6: the goddess Artemis might be seen as an archetypal image of the intrinsic hunger to find oneself through loneness,

> Philemon and the other figures of my fantasies brought home to me the crucial insight that there are things in the psyche which I do not produce, but which produce themselves and have their own life.
> ~ C.G. Jung[47]

specifically as a recluse enraptured by the natural world. Or you will read in Chapter 4 the way in which the archetypal image of Demeter and Persephone may symbolize the fluid relationship between a mother and daughter, each nurturing and nurtured by the other.

While Jung never employed the specific term *living image*, he often referenced psychic images, particularly archetypal images, describing them as "living entities which exert an attractive force upon the conscious mind."[48] These psychic images are dynamic, possessing a sense of aliveness and ability to render affect (meaning experienced emotionally) but only if they are encountered as autonomous. Jung saw these images as presenting both as figures and impulses, eidetic and felt as affect. To this end, he argued they must be engaged in some form of dialogue, suggesting interdependence and relationship between the self and these archetypal images with whom the self is engaging.

James Hillman, too, held that there was a responsibility upon us to be in relationship to them given the value they hold for the individual and collective psyche. In this relationship, the images are psychically alive. These images, understood as psychically alive, understood both as part of us and beyond us, move us toward our own wholeness. When images are seen and experienced as psychically alive, they are understood as animate. They are, as Hillman wrote, "the soul presenting itself straight on" because "images are the very stuff of our souls."[49]

To this point, let's consider the word *animate*. As a verb, it means to make alive, to bring to life. As an adjective, *animate* means to be alive or possessing life. By very definition, *animate* means living. Now consider the etymological roots of the word *animate*—*anima*—the Latin term for the word soul. In his seminal text, James Hillman stated that "we are in search of anima, or soul," which requires that we "save the phenomena of the imaginal psyche."[50] I argue that here Hillman is describing the living image: the animate, anima, soul-stuff, phenomenon of the psyche. What then about the spirit?

Numinous is the term that the theologian and philosopher Rudolph Otto coined to describe experiences of the divine.[51] Specifically, the psychiatrist Lionel Corbett saw such numinous phenomena as an experience of the archetypes, or, conversely, to experience an archetype is to experience that which is divine.[52] The inherent sovereignty of what is numinous allows for different imagistic manifestations of the Self (the archetype that is generally identified with the center *and* full scope of the personality, representing both the unity and plurality of the psyche including the many archetypes that evidence themselves through our lived experiences).

The Self, according to Corbett, may be imaged in Christ or Buddha, the Venus of Willendorf or crushed blades of grass, a silver fish or a many-breasted female giant, and so on. Its manifestation is tempered by the psychology of the individual for whom it manifests, where the connection of the personal (self) to the transpersonal (Self) is uniquely tailored. In other words, these archetypal images are animate and autonomous, choosing the ways in which they will approach each individual psyche. Archetypal images might then be considered as living images of the divine.

Let me unpack this idea. There is an affect associated with the experience of the archetype, and the intensity of that affect indicates the extent to which that experience has been embodied. This embodiment of the spirit, or the archetype, is what Lionel Corbett referred to as *the becoming of the soul.* In this way, what is transpersonal (spirit or archetype) becomes personal (soul) via an archetypal experience. This archetypal experience may

> The direct experience of spirit, or archetype, is always accompanied by an affect…the degree of affect indicates the degree of embodiment of the archetype, since affect is felt in the body…. when a spirit or archetype embodies, it takes on a personally meaningful quality which we call soul.
> ~ Lionel Corbett[53]

manifest as an intrapsychic image such that the self (personal) and the Self (transpersonal) interface in a way that consciousness might come to fathom the divine. The intrapsychic image as embodied spirit is living because it is a manifestation of the divine made available in an expression (an image) that holds the capacity to mediate the personal and the transpersonal. Through such interdependence, the soul is cultivated.

I know a woman who had a dream so profound that even when she described it to me some 40 years later, she said it still sent shivers up her spine. A child with poor sight and crossed-eyes, one night as she lay in her bed, she heard a booming voice and saw a bright light that assured her she would always see what truly mattered. She acknowledged it as the moment she knew she would someday leave her impoverished life, attend university, and go on to teach others, as she now does as an English professor. We might infer from her experience that the bright light and booming voice was some manifestation of an archetype, possibly the transpersonal Self, that sought to impact the self, forever changing this woman by growing her soul.

Thus, we understand from Lionel Corbett that the living image may be a sacred image. Animate and autonomous, this numinous image has the agency to engage the self in a way that may have the greatest impact on the psyche of that individual. Such engagement holds affect for this is the way it becomes embodied in order to make soul. Interestingly, research indicates that life events in which strong emotions are experienced, those high in affect, are the life events with the greatest power to be recalled—to become episodic, autobiographical memories.[54,55,56] It might be then that at least some of our memory-images are numinous. They are, perhaps, divine living images.

The American Indian scholar Vine Deloria, Jr. also saw such intrapsychic images as numinous. Deloria argued that these images which present themselves in visions or waking dreams are not just symbolic, something to be studied and interpreted; rather, they are living and autonomous, that which must be experienced. Deloria wrote, "Sioux dreams open up possibilities, for they offer evidence of the existence of a complex multi-layered universe in which meanings and energies existed that would eventually manifest themselves in the physical experiences."[57] For the Sioux, it would seem, psychic images are living—animate and autonomous and holding the wisdom to influence the dreamer both in the present and in the future.

Deloria supported this point in the examples he shared throughout his book. Specifically, he depicted how the Sioux accept that both the animals experienced in the physical realm and those met in the psychical realm offer wisdom especially as related to navigating the natural landscape. In fact, the Sioux believe that dream image animals must be accepted as having the same status as physical realm animals such that their wisdom be fully imparted and acted upon. Maybe you, like me, are thinking back to the idea raised earlier, that animals may also be psychopomps. The relationship developed with that animal depends upon listening and obeying messages from that animal received both in periods of waking and slumber. These psychical animal images hold the autonomous effort of carrying forth messages that the dreamer must obey not only for himself but for his greater community.

Let me give you an example of a woman I know who kept seeing a bear in her dreams. She understood from Native American teachings that the bear symbolized strength and power as well as healing, especially a healing of oneself that occurs in solitude. With courage, she embarked on a four-day vision quest, settling herself alone on the side of a mountain. One day, a mama and her baby bear entered her campsite. Startled, she shook the rattle she had brought with her, a gift from one of her most trusted teachers, to warn the bears of her presence. The next morning, she was unconvinced she had truly seen the bears, that is until both returned, again leaving her unharmed but now quite assured of their existence! Coupling her dreams with her experience in the wild, she came to believe not only was she right to come to this mountain to heal a generational wound, but it was her calling to take that healing out into the world, which she now does.

Deloria noted the reciprocity between the animal and the human, both gaining knowledge from the other.[58] Indeed, image and dreamer are in a reciprocal, interdependent relationship; both function as subject and object for the other, each existing as individual an entity. Deloria offered several anecdotes that depict this important interconnectedness. In the story of Black Elk, the Sioux medicine man sought to return to the psychic realm where his dream or vision imparted a reality other than that which he had previously known. Brave Buffalo, a Sioux elder, received powers directly from the dream images, where these powers carried over into the physical world that not only protected Brave Buffalo but also healed others. These images are living in part because they hold the ability to affect the dreamer in the psychical world as well as to affect the dreamer and others in the physical world.

Hmm, let's chew on that. Have you ever experienced a moment when you awoke from a dream and tried to straighten out whether you were mentally processing material from the dream world or the physical world? Jack Kerouac once surmised that dreams and memories are inextricable,[59] and I suspect he may have been on to something, but let me offer examples as a less esoteric way to understand the effect of our psychic materials. I have awoken from dreams of being in an argument with my husband Dan and literally being so angry with him when I awoke that I moved away from his sleeping body in a harrumph, physically separating us with pillows. I have a friend who once confessed to having a quite intimate and explicit dream-state rendezvous with a colleague such that, the next morning at work, she could not look him straight-faced in the eye. The lingering emotions of our dreams influence us despite our rational knowing that *it was only a dream.*

Returning to the psychic impact of dream animals, James Hillman too supported the recognition of dream animals as animate, seeing them as the transport of souls.[60] Thus, he argued, like Deloria, they not be interpreted but attentively observed and authentically engaged as we would with any real, living figure that enters our presence and requests our attention. When we allow these dream animal images, as Deloria and Hillman shared, to be in relationship with us, to offer and receive, we find that both we and the images hold the ability to transform.

I once dreamt that my dream-ego had stolen into my dream neighbor's house to go through her mail in search of her birthday card that my dream-ego had forgotten to send (of course this makes no sense, but our dreams often make no sense when we observe them from the physical world's perspective—all the more reason to engage with them imaginatively!). In waking from the dream and during its retelling, I *held* such humiliation for trespassing, but when the dream was tended by Stephen Aizenstat through the process of Dream Tending, and I witnessed the living images of the dream, I came to *feel* a deep sense of love and belonging.

It's hard to imagine how humiliation shifts to love and belonging, but it can when we meet psychic images just as they are and without any preconceived notions of what they should be, when we allow the body versus the mind to tell us how we feel. As the images shifted during the Dream Tending, I understood that the birthday card was my card, and the image of the little dog on its front cover became the psychic image of Little Black Dog, a little black terrier who imagistically licked at my hands and who intimated, through its imaginal presence, that it sought love and was the love of the higher self, or the transpersonal Self we discussed earlier. You might be interested to know, as I was, that the dog is often a psychopomp figure and the birthday card, being my card, suggested my own re-birth. Indeed, it was a critical time in my life as I was letting go of things that no longer served me and entering a new way of approaching myself and my life.

We've explored dream images as living, but what then can we say about memory-images, are they also living images? If we believe that memory-images are psychic images, a term more commonly associated to dream images, we might surmise that they could share the same inherent qualities or at least the potential of those qualities, namely that they may engage us at the deepest emotional levels, having lasting impressions upon the self because they are the stuff of the self and the soul.

To be clear, we aren't talking about all our memories, but consider why it is, some 40 years after we have experienced an event in our life, that we still may recollect it (collect it again) with rich eidetic and emotional detail. Why is it that I can still see my little hand offering the tab of a bandage through the window to my mother's soapy dish-hand for another safe passage along the concrete porch of my childhood home? Why is it, even as I type these words, that I am smiling for the warmth, peace, and love that this memory brings? Why is it that you surely can do the same? Might it be because they are quite alive in our psyches?

To build upon this argument, I turn to the philosopher Edward Casey whose study of memory and imagination offer a way in towards seeing memory-images also as living images.[61] I've already, in the previous chapter, discussed Casey's perspective regarding memory as image and a bedfellow of imagination, so I won't repeat myself here. What I wish to expound upon is the way in which Casey described the memory-image. He argued that these psychic images that represent our memory both portray matters of the past as well as *actively* imagine that past.

It is this activity I want to stress—this is not something passive or of simple causation; rather it is something with energetic purpose regardless of the implicit nature of that activity or purpose. Did I live, as a little child, in a small home with a concrete porch and a kitchen window that faced it? Yes, here my memory is portraying the past. Yet, when I re-call it, call it into conscious awareness, I am actively imaging the sweetness of my childhood, the warmth of my mother, and the glee of getting lost in my games of pretend. I seem to approach it with a hunger and find that it satiates me with a rush of energy and emotion though I can only guess as to why.

What's more, Casey explained that for these memory-images to exist at all, they must be allowed to transcend the limitations of the past, escaping any physical or temporal fixedness. They must be vibrant, alive with meaning and emotion, so that they may resonate, reverberate, and resound within us. This resounding, literally a re-sounding, a hearing again and perhaps in a new form, dislodges these memory-images from the confines of their lived experience. They are neither the whimsical musings of pure imagination nor are they static vestiges of a fixed and immutable past. In this way, they emerge as having their own intention and authority independent of the original life experience they would otherwise seem to re-present. They have a life of their own! Memory-images are, in my own words, living images if for no other reason than that they *come to us* this way—they present to our psyches as animate, autonomous, and wise. We would do well to treat them as such as the following story suggests.

In my first encounter with imaginal remembering, I had the privilege of working with a woman who is sixty-some years old; Liora is an elegant woman, with silver white hair. She is simultaneously direct and diminutive, finding a way to speak her truth without diminishing anyone else's.

One afternoon, as we walked along a dusty gravel road in the mountains of Montana, I mustered up the courage to share with her my idea that perhaps memories are images and might be engaged imaginally. Liora was the second person with whom I'd shared the notion of imaginal remembering (the first was originally aghast at such an idea, though she has since shifted, now being one of imaginal remembering's biggest champions). To my great surprise and delight, Liora stopped along the road, turned to me, looked me straight in the eyes, and shared a memory which she wanted to engage in this way.

When Liora was a young girl, she was raised by her nanny, Marjorie, because Liora's single mother worked long hours to earn enough to care for her three daughters after Liora's father and step-father had passed. Liora and I agreed to meet each other by phone once we'd both returned home from Montana. One late autumn afternoon, I phoned her, and together, we invited her memory to be imaginally engaged.

Liora recalled sitting on the front-porch steps of her Midwestern home, a child of about five years with soft blond curls. She sat on those steps with Marjorie as they awaited Marjorie's taxi that would take her to the other side of their little Midwest town. In the memory, Liora asks Marjorie, "Where did you come from?" Marjorie replies, "Don't you never mind about that," trying to send Liora off with a coin to buy a popsicle.

"Where did you come from" indeed, for as Liora had already explained to me, Marjorie was a black woman, with a strange dialect, who lived on the black side of town. Liora remembers little of Marjorie outside of her role as caretaker, but she knew that Marjorie wore hats and attended church each Sunday, her one day off. Being in deep relationship with a person of color was something Liora had little other experience with as a child of the 1950s growing up in the Midwest. Thus, the question and the curiosity—"Where did you come from?"

She remembered sitting on those concrete steps and wanting to reach out with her tiny hand and touch the chocolate skin of Marjorie, to make physical connection with this woman whom Liora so loved and sought love from in return. Yet, Marjorie would not have allowed such touch. Working long hours, taking care of Liora and her sisters, might have involved healthy meals, but it did not come with hugs and kisses. Not in those days and in that town.

Though Liora entered the memory-image wishing to touch the Marjorie-image, she was careful not to do so for fear that the image would dissolve, leaving Liora alone there on the steps of her memory. Yet, in her patience and openness, the re-collected physical Marjorie-image, invited a second Marjorie (Church-Going Marjorie), and then a third (Spirit Marjorie). This glowing spirit is perhaps a manifestation of the divine, specifically the divine presence of the higher self that is present within Liora.

It is this Spirit Marjorie who makes a deep connection with Liora some sixty years after the original event, allowing touch, returning laughter, and offering love. "I am feeling very peaceful at this moment," Liora shared of her experience. "When I let the Spirit Marjorie come in, then she loves me. I see in her central nature how much she loves me and that it's okay for me to touch her. In this moment, it is a really nice feeling, to almost lose her and then have her spiritual person come and join the person she was then." Spirit Marjorie is touchable and touched, loving and loveable, a contrast to the woman Liora recalls from years ago.

Liora questions the three Marjories about why there was no connection during their physical world time together, why Marjorie withheld love. Each Marjorie responds in like kind, "Why are you even asking that question? Don't you know I loved you, and that's what you are really asking? So why are you really asking?" Liora then imagines the ways in which the physical world Marjorie, a black woman from the other side of town, could and did show love: through well-balanced meals, quiet conversations, and clean clothes.

In this moment, Liora recognizes her expectations, conformations, and demands of love. "I expect somebody will express to me their love in a certain way . . . when all the time the person might be showing love all these different ways . . . the little girl in me wants to say, 'tell me you love me, do something warm and fuzzy to show me you love me.'"

For Liora, engaging in the memory imaginally engaged her in a deep conversation with her soul. What Liora demanded from Marjorie was not what her soul needed. She realized her soul seeks love, not a particular type of love, or a particular way of love, but simply love. These three Marjorie-images teach this to Liora. In turn, Liora learns to accept love more fully and more openly.

Returning more than 60 years into her past, Liora learned something about her current self and how she wished to be in the future, who she wanted to be as her future self. In part, this experience prompted Liora's current dedication of time and effort to the Race Equity Coalition. From Liora and my perspectives, imaginal remembering is a work of and for the soul.

The living image, I believe, *is a living image* because *we choose to approach it as such*. These images of our psyche will meet us as we meet them, engaging with us as animate and autonomous when we are willing to receive them in this way.

This description of the living image, focused on a *how* rather than a *what*, eludes the reductionist dictates of a modern culture that demands a definition which points back to something measurable and generalizable. *Living* need not require physical presence—a fleshy, breathing body that would fog up the mirrors of our world. In the worldview I'm

> Let go of earlier associations or connections to the image, and instead allow its living presence to further open your own. Experience the wonder of this encounter as you would a wordless meeting with a beloved friend.
> ~ Stephen Aizenstat[62]

suggesting, these images mirror all the same because they are mirrors of the psyche. Whether from imagination, dreams, or memories, they are psychically real, moving of their own choice and from their own intelligence because our approach to them acknowledges that though they may touch our ego, they also extend well beyond it. These images live in the deepest recesses of our own psyche but also, as we have discussed, they are a part of the transpersonal psyche, that collective unconscious tied to the soul of the world.

CHAPTER 4

APPROACHING THE LIVING IMAGES

The French philosopher Gaston Bachelard held high esteem for the images of our psyche.[63] He described their youthful and naïve nature as if describing a child not yet conformed and tainted by the expectations and critiques of the external world. From this perspective, he described a kind of phenomenology that would hold itself to observing the image as it first emerges. Only in its primacy, before colored by the interpretations of the ego and the culture in which the ego serves, might we witness the full measure, strength, and multiplicity of the image. Thus, he argued, the phenomenology-of-the-image, the way in which we approach, observe, and/or engage with the image would not be mistaken as a phenomenology-of-the-mind.

Rather, the phenomenology-of-the-image is poetic, and thereby, a phenomenology-of-the-soul. If we flip this around, we might then see it from the vantage that poetry as a phenomenology-of-the-soul implies a poetic approach to the image, a perspective of the image as imaginatively, emotionally, sensuously, and metaphorically expressive. Liora's example in the previous chapter helps us to see this difference. The mind would not allow Liora to touch the memory-image of the physical world Marjorie, so it would seem the soul

invited Spirit Marjorie, the Marjorie who is open to and returning of
Liora's loving touch.

Taking a step back, let's begin by seeing the phenomenology-of-
the-image as a theoretical framework seated within the broader
discussion of phenomenology. Bear with me, as this gets a little
heady. Initiated by German philosopher Edmund Husserl,
phenomenology as a philosophical movement began at least in part
as an attempt to mediate empiricism (knowledge derived from
sensory experience) and rationalism (knowledge derived from
reason), finding neither to be a satisfying explanation for the human
experience.[64]

Phenomenology called attention to the notions of object and
subject (terms exploited by the hard sciences) as being merely
philosophical constructs that misconstrue the way in which humans
experience the world. In response, phenomenology sought to offer a
holistic approach that accepted a relationship between the object and
the subject because it accepted that any conscious experience is
naturally a comingling of the object with the one who experiences it.
We'll get to an example in a moment, but let's get through the theory.

Edmund Husserl was not arguing against the notions of subject
and object per se; rather, he was challenging the sciences to recognize
that their primary platform of discovery—a subject-object divide—
doesn't exist. Indeed, the subject knows the object through the
subject's experience of that object. What this means is that the
subject cannot be separate completely from the object because any
conscious awareness of the object is pulled through the lens of the
subject. Abstract, I know.

Here's what I'm getting at: Husserl was arguing for an
understanding of and speaking to the *essence* of the experience which
creates the connectedness between object and consciousness. He
believed that from such essence much can be inferred. What I'm
suggesting is that Husserl was encouraging a way of seeing each
experience (an act of consciousness interfacing with object) as a
phenomenon ingrained with a pure essence and worthwhile of
exploration and understanding. Naturally, this includes the
phenomenon of encountering psychic images.

Indeed, C.G. Jung wrote that "every psychic process is an image
and an 'imagining,' otherwise no consciousness could exist and the
occurrence would lack phenomenality."[65] It's as if Jung rebuked any

question of whether without image and imagining there would be consciousness whatsoever. Thus, phenomenology is, first and foremost, phenomenology-of-the-image, for without the image there would be no consciousness of the object, no experience of the experienced.

Let me try to explain this with a simple example. As I type these words, there is a cup of tea sitting by me. I (subject) understand the cup (object) because of my prior encounters with similar cups of tea. The image of the cup is a psychic reflection of my experiences with cups. For example, I may imagine this cup, like others I've encountered in the past, will hold its hot liquid contents until I place my lips at its rim and tip it towards my mouth. If someone were to ask me to explain a teacup, I couldn't without drawing upon my own psychic image and imaginings of experiences with teacups. If you're holding a cup of tea now as you read these words, I can imagine it, and your experiences with it, from my own experiences with my teacups. My thoughts, feelings, memories, and even dreams that involve teacups draw upon my images of them. Therefore, we draw upon our own psychic images and imaginings (even as comparisons to similar images) to make sense of the objects (things or experiences) of our world.

Phenomenology-of-the-Image as a Practice

The question then becomes how do we do this? How do we engage with the image to experience it as a phenomenon that we grasp and accept? Let's begin by considering what it means to be a phenomenologist of the image.

Psychologist Mary Watkins outlined what I see as a phenomenological approach to the imaginal that was in part founded upon and supported by fiction writers, including playwrights and novelists.[66] She argued that many of those authors who introduce their readers to the richest, deepest, seemingly most real characters, approach those characters as if they're autonomous. In other words, the characters are not developments of the author's ego. Rather the characters are wholly other than the ego, where the author bears witness to these imaginal figures. When we read a book like Alice

Walker's *The Color Purple* or F. Scott Fitzgerald's *The Great Gatsby*, the characters come alive to us. We can see them in our minds' eyes as we read the words on the page, watching them as if we're flies on their imaginary walls. We even wish to know how their lives turned out like a dear friend or lover we lost touch with years ago. When we part ways with them, as we turn to close the cover of the book, we think of them as continuing, somewhere, somehow.

As Watkins describes them, writers like Walker and Fitzgerald seem to be the quintessential phenomenologists. They stay close to the phenomena studied, carefully observing them without purposefully interpreting them. It would seem they understand the importance of holding notable curiosity and necessary detachment from the characters to allow the characters to fully develop. In this approach, the writer can be even left astonished by what he witnesses of the character because the author does not govern the character.

As phenomenologists, the writers take careful note of the characters with whom they engage without directing or interpreting their actions based upon the authors' ego-perspectives. Rather, the authors of these deeply developed characters approach the characters as holding their own autonomy, subsequently allowing these characters, reciprocally, to approach them. In other words, the character and its presentation to the author aren't specifically in service to the author's ego.

From a psychoanalytic perspective, Mary Watkins referred to this type of approach, one in which the ego is of equal status to the image, neither being supreme in knowledge nor in power, as that of the "'observing ego'" or the "internal observer."[67] Watkins was careful to make a distinction between the ego that is lost to psychosis and the ego that can hold a realistic stance toward the image, recognizing that the image-figure is not physically present.

I would argue that this observing ego is the ego of the phenomenologist, carefully observing the imaginal figure as distinct from the figures of the physical world. This ego requires a wisdom, flexibility, temperance, and empathy that are generally developed in the practice of engaging with the images. The observing ego is a phenomenologist's ego that, through practice, can shift away from a purely egoistic approach to phenomena.

There seem to be ways in which to call upon the observing ego so that we may engage as phenomenologists of the image. Before moving into the very practical approach from which imaginal remembering was developed, let's review some general approaches to engaging with the images of our psyche.

To begin, there is a plethora of literature and practical guidance available regarding the Eastern practices of meditation. Foundational to this practice is the acknowledgment that before we can soften the ego, we must first attend to our bodies and quiet the mind. Many meditation styles teach us first to become aware of the images and voices that regularly float to the surface of our mind, and second, without judgement, to allow them to drift away. It's not that we necessarily fight for an imageless, dialogue-free mind (for such warring would only further agitate the ego). Rather, meditation invites us to become aware of our ego's conversations with these images and voices so that we can quiet the ego's part in what may, at times, seem like ceaseless chatter within the mind.

Adopting this into our own practice of preparing ourselves for an engagement with the imaginal, by softening the ego, we invite the heightened sensitivity of the observing ego. We also lessen the chatter of our mind and the eagerness of our ego to step into a directive or interpretive role with the image. This heightened sensitivity, coupled with a softened ego, encourage a somatic attendance wherein the body is primed to feel into the affect of engaging with the image.

In some ways, this takes, according to James Hillman, a freeing of our senses from the confines of the physical realm, allowing them to move toward their soulful capabilities.[68] The senses—sight, smell, sound, touch, and taste—as we have come to typically rely on them, aren't the most relevant ways to encounter imaginal phenomena. This is because, in a way, we've become "imaginatively" dull in our over-emphasis on locating the five senses in the physical world only. If we cannot sense the imaginal world, we narrow its phenomena and the wisdom it might otherwise offer. For example, if we remember a gardenia in our grandmother's garden, we may not think to describe its smell, because it's "just a memory" or "just in my imagination." Yet, we might miss rich metaphorical meanings that such a sense image would relate. Is the gardenia yellowed, smelling of rot? Or is it bright white, at the peak of its perfumery? The scent matters to the memory-image's meaning.

Our senses are ingrained with intuitive power and introspective capacity. They can sense what is happening *within us* somatically and intrapsychically. Have you ever heard something that made you shiver for no apparent reason? Have you ever smelled an aroma that suddenly prompted you to recall the otherwise forgotten dream you had the night before? Our senses need only be retrained back toward their intuitive sensibility to meaningfully approach the images of our psyche. The notion of *sticking to the image* invites the image to be imbued with all that it is and all that it touches rather than just by plucking the image from its context and assigning it an egoic or cultural meaning.

For example, if we dream of a snake, we might immediately assume it means temptation or rebirth or evil or fertility or any number of things through our associations and amplifications. But when we approach it and its context fully, from all our senses, the meaning of its presence becomes both expansive and precise. We might begin by perceiving the snake image from the way in which our physical realm would have us, through our senses.

Starting with our eyes, we watch the way and the medium upon which the snake moves, perhaps noticing its dry, smooth scales that slither against the cold marble floor of our dream home. We see its red, yellow, and black stripes, and then, bringing in our ears, we might hear, ever so slightly, it serpentine along the marble. We could leave it at that, approaching the snake image from just the way our senses have been prompted to meet our physical world. But Hillman argued we should twist and turn the senses, perceiving the snake image with an intuitive and introspective capacity.

> An image is not what you see but the way you see.
> ~ James Hillman[69]

Through imagination, we enter the snake. We move from observing it at a distance to becoming the snake. We begin to feel ourselves as the snake, slithering our dry scales along the cold floor. Embodying its movements makes us vividly aware that our own movements in life have become dry and cold, prompting us to wonder where the passion has gone. We see the red, yellow, and black of the snake-image and begin to dress our own psychic bodies in these vivid alchemical colors until we are clothed in the wisdom that life is a continual death-rebirth process. We become the snake's forked tongue flicking at the air, understanding it is our own most sensitive selves that must probe what lies ahead.

Hillman argued we are already doing just this type of sensory intuition though often quite unaware. Turning things in upon themselves, as he often did, he challenged our perception of the word "sense"; he noted that we use this word as much to express an approach to the physical realm (your keen sense of hearing) as we do for our intuitive faculties (I sense that you understand what I mean).

He argued that our cultural idioms belie the physical world senses; for example, we smell something fishy when we are skeptical about a person or a circumstance. When we get a taste of our own medicine, we experience the bitterness of being judged or directed as we have judged or directed others. When we pull these same five senses through our intuitive palates, through our poetic dispositions, we sense the psychic images not just as *the what* of our experience but in *the how* that we experience them. In this way, we engage with the images as the images seek to engage with us, presenting themselves to us precisely and fully as they are.

C.G. Jung offered a practical approach when he described the process of *active imagination*; it might at first appear as simplistic but is a rather careful, unfettered way of attending to the image. Specifically, he counseled one to be patient and perceptive with the image. He further advised to avoid fickleness, leaping from one image to the other. The image will, of its own accord and in its own time, shift. Once this mode of careful observation is established, then

> Contemplate [the image] and carefully observe how the picture begins to unfold or to change. Don't try to make it into something, just do nothing but observe what its spontaneous changes are.
> ~ C.G. Jung[70]

one can more intimately approach the image, becoming a participant in its environment and, eventually, engaging with the image directly perhaps through dialogue.

By moving delicately, with attentiveness and patience, the image itself also seems to soften, unfolding into that which is more open, more inviting. In other words, there's a preparation that's required to allow ourselves, perhaps more aptly stated, to allow our egos, to sit in stillness and in waiting. And in this waiting that yields to openness, our ego shifts to one of the observing ego that holds a phenomenological approach to the image.

The Purpose and Practice of Dreamwork

Now we move to the specifics, the guided way in which one might approach a memory-image, what I call the process of imaginal remembering. As I have hinted, this process is based on the practice of dreamwork, most specifically Dream Tending, which was developed by Stephen Aizenstat and is, itself, based on the dreamwork of other depth psychologists and shamans.

Before we begin, let me explain that I do not define dreams as something that occurs during slumber only. As I've previously discussed, dreaming extends into the daylight hours in ways that, for example, Mary Watkins described as waking dreams,[71] the Jungian analyst Robert Johnson described as inner work,[72] and Vine Deloria, Jr. described as visions.[73] Lionel Corbett was clear throughout his writing that intrapsychic images are not only those experienced during nocturnal states but also in waking dreams and other forms of numinous experiences such as in somatic affect, through engagement with nature, and during psychotherapy.[74] Dreams are the language of psyche, and, as I discuss below, they may even manifest as disease, both physical and psychological. Stephen Aizenstat shared that "everything is dreaming," and even in the mirror of nature we see the wild world as a dream in its reflection of psyche.[75]

In these ways, dreamwork extends beyond working with just dream images that visit us in our sleep. Rather, dreamwork is a way in which we are in relationship with the psyche; perhaps then we more broadly describe dreamwork as self-work. When we hold in awareness and curiosity the images of our psyche as they present to us in dreams, conversations held with others, our encounters in and with nature, and the recollections of our past, we gift ourselves the opportunities to know better who we are and perhaps where we are going. It is for this reason, as I describe the purposes and practices of dreamwork in general and Dream Tending in specific, I am describing the ways in which I have engaged personally and with others in the practice of imaginal remembering.

When I use the term *purpose*, I feel immediately called to clarify. What I do *not* mean by purpose is a rational goal indubitably resulting in a preconceived something. Neither do I mean a fixed determination towards a material outcome. What I do mean is that low vibration that seems to energize our efforts, that gentle breeze that floats us along our intended paths, whatever those paths might be or mean.

That breeze and those paths, for Stephen Aizenstat, had something to do with the way in which dreams changed the dreamers' lives. In his seminal text that fully describes the process and the power of Dream Tending, he wrote, "The more deeply I listened to dream figures, the more my clients experienced positive changes in their lives. . . . As their dreams came alive, so did each person's sense of self worth."[76]
Aizenstat wrote of witnessing an interdependency between dreamer and image that yields to the potential for psychological healing. Just by listening, something powerful has the possibility of occurring. Our

> When we rush in too quickly with our bright ideas of what the image means, we rob it of its native intelligence and replace it with our own, which may not be as illuminating.
> ~ Stephen Aizenstat[77]

ego might assume the need to act, yet that impression seems to be an outcropping of our modern culture's obsession with productivity, where productivity in terms of dreamwork could be as innocent as rushing towards an interpretation of the dream images. But that rushing diminishes the image and the wisdom that it might offer.

Let's return to the snake we spoke about earlier in this chapter. You could dream of this snake, for example, and immediately decide the snake means temptation and start looking in your life for where you might be tempted. But you might just witness the snake-image, inviting it into your imagination to see what message it might have to share. I've been caught off guard by the messages of my intrapsychic images.

Likewise, I've met many a dreamer who spent time with the most dreadful of dream images only to find that these monsters, in the end, turned out to offer the greatest support and wisdom. As the saying goes, if it surprises you, you can be more assured it wasn't the ego talking. Ironically, then, it's not by way of arduous exertion but by way of our simple yet deeply reverent presence to the images, that we're most capable of listening deeply to and learning from these psychic images.

Though there's been much written regarding direct outcomes of working with the images of our psyche, I want to focus our intention on the idea that the less we foreclose on the results of our efforts, the greater the potential return. In working with memory-images in the process of imaginal remembering, I find that when no expectation is outlined, the outcome of the experience is quite meaningful and often unexpected.

Stephen Aizenstat began his guidebook, *Dream Tending: Awakening the Healing Power of Dreams*, by outlining those individuals, texts, and experiences that influenced the development and refinement of Dream Tending as a practice of dreamwork. First and perhaps foremost, Aizenstat credited his great-grandfather Zadie, a man from the old world who "believed that beneath the rational mind there exists a spirit that feeds our essential humanity and is part of a larger spiritual truth."[78] Zadie came to recognize this "wild, beautiful and brilliant life force that is the essence of all things" as "the truth that guided his entire life."

It is worthy to note that a dream brought Aizenstat back into relationship with Zadie (many years after his great-grandfather had passed). The dream led Aizenstat to what would become a deep understanding of and relationship to dreams that, in my interpretation, are manifestations of this life force. The dream specifically called Aizenstat to a physically real book, a manual really, that held Zadie's ancient and experientially earned wisdom.

Stephen Aizenstat also credited Sigmund Freud, C.G. Jung, and James Hillman for guiding his development of Dream Tending, which is based on three distinct but complementary methods of working with dream images: association, amplification, and animation. Thus, I speak to Aizenstat's perspective of these influences as well as share my own understanding of these authors' (and a few others') texts to help expand or dimensionalize the practice of Dream Tending especially as it relates to imaginal remembering.

Association

To begin, Stephen Aizenstat credited the method of association (for example, seeing the dream snake as signifying one's physical world temptation towards an adulterous affair) to Sigmund Freud who believed that dreamwork simply requires effective detective skills, uncovering the hidden meanings that masquerade as symbolic imagery.[79] Implicit in Freud's

> Every dream has a meaning, though a hidden one . . . we have only to undo the substitution correctly in order to arrive at this hidden meaning.
> ~ Sigmund Freud[80]

perspective of dreams are the notions that (1) a dream has a clear and distinct meaning, and (2) understanding that meaning is a process of decoding.

Thus, Freud's writings offer many examples of decoded psychic images deciphered into precise day-world objects and experiences that are rife with unpalatable meanings (and ergo hidden from the dreamer). For instance, if a male dreamer exchanges flowers with a female in a dream, it might suggest the male dreamer wishes to deflower her, to take her virginity, in the physical world.

To this end, Stephen Aizenstat encouraged the method of association, seeing it as a method that is most closely *associated* to the ego[81]—that part of ourselves more identifiable to our waking lives and the way we move in the physical world. The purpose of the association method is to find the implicit connections between the images of our dreams and the realities of our physical realm.

Aizenstat offered an example of association: the dream figure of a lion. The dream lion might be associated with the physical realm experiences of a trip to the zoo, National Geographic, a jerk of a boss, or a combative father. The last two, might then, point toward one's own rage, suppressed or expressed. Through such associations, the dreamer may come to understand that the unconscious, through psychic imagery, is aiding our ability to release stored emotion repressed by the ego. Robert Johnson in *Inner Work* offered this approach as well, suggesting the use of a mind-map that diagrammatically moves one associated term to the next, weaving an interconnection of meanings.[82]

At this point, it may be valuable to raise a counter-perspective to the method of association. The method of association, that stays close to the ego, would, based on what we have already explored, seem to diminish the image, its inherent animation, and its autonomy, where we run the danger of reducing the image to "nothing but" our fathers, our bosses, or a reminder of a trip to the zoo. While this may be true, especially if association is the only approach ever used, it still can be meaningful. I do believe that some images are speaking directly to our ego and an ego-approach toward them may be just, especially if it is also coupled with other approaches.

The method of association, while it may be reductive, does the work of recognizing the psychic image as relying on physically real phenomena to express its meaning(s). Thus, in working with memories, which are grounded in some physical reality, I take heart in acknowledging that modern depth psychology's original approach to dreams accepted that our day world phenomena, our physical world experiences, are imaginatively disguised by our psyche such to make them bearable to our egos. This suggests our memories may undertake a similar imaginative veiling.

Further, despite my reverence toward the imaginal, I realize the importance of the ego and its needs. There is great learning to be had when one passes through the lens of the ego, this being as true for memory as it for dreams. We know our memories are highly influenced by our current self, and this self highly influences our ego. The method of association, then, being closest to the ego, may offer worthwhile reflection regarding what our memories share with us about the current self, especially as that self lives in relationship to the past.

For this reason, and as you'll see in the chapters that follow, when I work with individuals using imaginal remembering, we initially explore the memory through the ego's associations. Such grounding seems important to the work that follows, not least of which because it seems to offer a threshold between the physical and psychical realms.

Amplification

Stephen Aizenstat credited C.G. Jung with the second method of working with dreams and psychic images—amplification. The dream snake here can be amplified, via the Old Testament, as the temptation that leads us to the tree of knowledge, where the chthonic aspects of our own nature and nature itself drive us toward whatever grounding wisdom we need or seek.

Indeed, it was Jung who believed that some psychic images emerge from the collective unconscious, that limitless area of the shared psyche.[83] The most meaningful dreams, those dreams that affect not only the dreamer but the *anima mundi*, the world soul, emerge from the collective unconscious. This collective unconscious is like a very animated, bustling ever-morphing warehouse that, among other things, stores relevant remnants from ancient to current myths, folklore, and religions, making images from these sources available to our individual psyches in ways that help us to understand and connect to the transpersonal psyche or collective consciousness. In this way, Jung saw that these psychic images extend beyond our own personal, egoic associations. Rather, these images are often the manifestations of primordial patterns or archetypes that are relevant to each individual as a part of the transpersonal psyche.

Let's take the moon as an example. For me, a full moon image could be associated to the time in which I spent four days and nights alone of the side of the mountain. I longed for the moon to quickly make its way across the star-filled sky each night so that sunlight would return, and I would see the world around me and not feel quite so alone. But the moon, when amplified, can suggest something quite archetypal and universal: it is the feminine to the masculine sun, that which is the fertile, the mutable, the watery, the emotional, the irrational, and the depths of the unconscious. It is both protective and dangerous, imaginative and intuitive.[84] Amplified, the moon in my dream may share the same symbolic overtures as the moon in your dream. Though strangers, we are connected by its archetypal significance. Thus, the anima mundi, the world's soul, is a fabric woven of these deep, ancient, and universal threads that bind us all.

For Jung, these psychic images appear at key periods during an individual's individuation process (the life-long process of becoming who we are intended to be). For example, images of the moon might show up in the life of a woman who is pregnant with an idea of where her life may lead. Through the image of the moon, the collective unconscious may be nudging her to leave something safe and well-developed for what is nascent and ill-defined. In this practice of individuation, the ego works toward the conscious awareness that it is only one part of the psyche's totality, only one component of a much greater whole. In our moon example, this woman's ego must let go of what is fixed and prudent, so that the soul, guided by the higher self, can journey onward.

Robert Johnson saw archetypal amplification as an extension of association because he recognized that the archetypal images manifest in a way that is personal to the dreamer. It is key that the individual understands the way in which the archetype is connecting directly with her life so that the dreamwork has meaning. The woman, met by images of the moon, might not connect with the watery, irrational aspects of the archetypal moon but with the feminine, fertility aspects.

> Every symbol in your dream has a special, individual connotation that belongs to you alone, just as the dream is ultimately yours alone.
> ~ Robert Johnson[85]

Thus, amplification is still connected in a way that is personal, rather than wholly transpersonal, such that she can still be impacted by her presence to the moon-image. In a similar way, Stephen Aizenstat believed that the method of amplification extends the symbol to its richest archetypal capacity and then examines how that archetype is actively present in the life of the dreamer.[86] We see that even though the process of amplification takes us beyond our own personal associations, there's still a deep personal connection we have with these psychic images; in fact, without such connection the amplification method renders itself meaningless. No matter how many times you tell the woman that the moon in mythology represents what is mutable and irrational, if that doesn't resonate with her, it's not a meaningful connection.

Lionel Corbett's texts offer some excellent examples regarding the technique of amplification as holding the capacity to express a personal meaning through collective symbolism. One illustration regards a young psychiatric resident who dreams of sitting with her two brothers on a bed and feeling honey that drips upon her from a lioness suspended above. When Corbett worked with the woman and her dream, he shared with her the Biblical story of Samson who happened upon a "'swarm of bees and honey'. . . in the carcass of a lion."[87] He also amplified the dream as speaking through the Greek

Goddess Demeter as the great mother who is "depicted as a bee" as well as a "lioness."

As is often the case, these religious/mythological symbols were consciously and personally unknown to the dreamer. However, through the process of amplification, Corbett found that the transpersonal (archetype) interfaced with the personal (self) for Corbett believed the dream suggested, among other things, that the dreamer embrace her chosen career of psychiatry from the archetype of the feminine. Despite that the symbols were originally unconscious to the dreamer, the symbolic manifestation of the collective had a personal and direct meaning and implication for her once the symbolic meaning of these images was made conscious.

I had the opportunity to imaginally remember with a middle-aged woman, Rachel, whose mother had attempted suicide when the woman was a teen. She first described the memory as she recalled it. Then, as is done in imaginal remembering, she entered the memory as an image and engaged with it as such. The woman recognized both historic details and distortions during the imaginal remembering experience. Strikingly, the mother memory-image appeared as an adolescent girl whom the woman cuddled on the floor, singing to and rocking (a startling image as it was quite distinct from her historical memory). Working with the memory-images by way of amplification invited in the Greek myth of Demeter and Persephone.

You may recall that in the myth, the daughter is stolen away, the one whose life is forever changed by a tragic event. Yet the daughter must console, must mother her mother. The myth helps us to understand the fluidity of mother and daughter, of maiden and crone, seeing that as daughters, we are beholden to our mothers as both children and nurturers.

After engaging with it, the woman reflected on the memory-image. She intuited that the roles of mother and daughter had been shifted, understanding an inherent fluidity in the relationship she had and still has with her mother. By amplifying the mythical symbols, the woman found personal associations; as Robert Johnson suggested, the transpersonal mediated the personal.[88]

To personify our life stories, as James Hillman recommended, seeing through our own lives to the archetypal images that stand behind them, encourages us to see our own experiences in a deeply transpersonal and interconnected way.[89] It allows us to see that our life experiences, such as the sometimes need for daughters to mother their mothers, are both ours individually and ours collectively; they are our personal stories as well as the universal stories stored in the warehouse of myths.

Animation

The method of animation is arguably the most profound and most critical of all three methods to the practice of imaginal remembering because it hinges on the fundamental belief in the living images of our psyche. The practice of engaging with the animated images of our psyche was referred to by Jung as *active imagination* and is well illustrated in C.G. Jung's *The Red Book: Liber Novus.*[90] This text captures the images painted and words written about Jung's *nekyia,* his journey into the unconscious. Curiously, it seems that his childhood memories first drew Jung into the practice of active imagination, the practice that would

> My actual experiences of the unconscious taught me that such contents are not dead, outmoded forms, but belong to our living being.
> ~ C.G. Jung[91]

move him away from the Freudian perspective of a more reductive and fixed approach to the unconscious and towards an engagement with these images as if they were still filled with life and animated as such.

He explained in his memoir *Memories, Dreams, Reflections* that in attempting to work through his own psychological dilemmas, he softened the ego and listened for the other voices of the psyche.

> The first thing that came to the surface was a childhood memory from perhaps my tenth or eleventh year. At that time, I had had a spell of playing passionately with building blocks. I distinctly recalled how I had built little houses and castles, using bottles to form the sides of gates and vaults. Somewhat later I had used ordinary stones, with mud and mortar. These structures had fascinated me for a long time. To my astonishment, this memory was accompanied by a good deal of emotion. "Aha," I said to myself, "there is still life in these things. The small boy is still around, and possesses a creative life which I lack. But how can I make

my way to it?" . . . This was a turning point in my fate, but I gave in only after endless resistances and with a sense of resignation.[92]

Not only did Jung turn away, albeit reluctantly, from his original stance that memories are something static and bygone, he recognized them as alive. It is at this point that Jung entered a period of deep engagement with the unconscious and began development and practice of active imagination, a technique from which Jung claimed all his other theories emerged.[93] It all began by an attentive engagement with a childhood memory that Jung realized was imbued with life.

This technique of active imagination, presenting oneself to one's imagination with openness and attentiveness, allowing it to take us places beyond the ego's control, this is the basis for imaginal remembering. You will read more below about the practice of active imagination when I share the signposts of Dream Tending since Jung didn't so much offer his readers *how* to practice, but rather *why* to practice.

James Hillman expanded and deepened Jung's work by offering a way of understanding these images, taking them in as both their *what* and their *how*. Railing against any position that held psychic images as fixed, Hillman argued that many images, especially those of Christianity, died because their autonomous quality dried up as they were plucked away from the fertile soil of imagination. Pulled

> Image-work is directed to imagination and by imagination so that if healing comes, it comes through the middle realm of the psyche, a healing of the imaginal body.
> ~ James Hillman[94]

into an allegoric state, literalized by way of stipulating their "hidden" meaning, they were rendered inert in terms of our ability to connect with them.

We might think here of the image of the cross which is notably prevalent in our Western society as jewelry that anoints our ears, chests, and wrists. This cross, which is common among many ancient traditions, is pregnant with a multitude of meanings. It may symbolize unity and plurality, one thing that is also everything—two lines with four points that reach in different directions creating diameters of a circle or oval, shapes without beginning or ending.

However, among some Christians, it has been restricted to only representing their religion, and specifically, the way in which Jesus died, whereas the cross's rich, multifaceted meaning is lost.

In contrast to such a limited approach, Hillman argued that the proper means toward the image is to "turn to [it] with dulia, an attitude of service" rather than "lateria," which holds the image as an idol, closing it down to a fixed meaning.[95] When we meet these psychic images with a stance of what can they do for us or how they best serve religious dogma, much is lost. Rather, if we come to them imaginally, from the soul, with delicacy and patience, much more than we anticipated is often realized.

C.G. Jung and James Hillman wrote often of the outcome of animation, what it means to our psyche and soul when we engage with our intrapsychic images in this way. But I would argue that Stephen Aizenstat offered us the clearer approach regarding how to invite these images as animate and autonomous beings into our conscious awareness. This imaginal, embodied approach to the image was critical for Aizenstat as well.[96] He articulated "four fundamental attitudes" for the practice of Dream Tending: (1) Meet the Dream in the Way of the Dream; (2) Open Body Awareness; (3) Become Present in the Here and Now; and, (4) Engage the Dream in an Attitude of Not Knowing.

To meet the dream in the way of the dream, one must suspend the desires of the ego and approach the image poetically, from the soul, rather than the mind, as Gaston Bachelard so aptly expressed. In this way, we meet the image not in a way that demands an outcome but purely desires to be in the presence of the image, openly curious. In other words, the dream has its own approach, its own sensuality and sense of being. To approach the psychic image in the ways of the physical world is to ignore that the image is entirely its own phenomenon.

Second, and in complement to the first, the psychic image must be met with open body awareness. To a large extent, Stephen Aizenstat credited Marion Woodman, a Jungian analyst, with a deep reverence for the somatic embodiment of and thereby wisdom imparted from dream images. Aizenstat recommended an almost meditative approach to entering the imaginal not unlike the Eastern practice of meditation shared earlier in this chapter. Grounding to the earth and careful attentive breathing are approaches of coming into the body that move us toward open body awareness for the living image and help us become fully present. This grounding to the body is the way we come into what Aizenstat referred to as the *archetypal ego* or the *essential self* which represents our deepest, most authentic nature.

Though Aizenstat argued that the archetypal ego is in some ways different from the Self, a concept that has been explored earlier in this book, I believe there are notable similarities. Given that the Self is described as the unity and the multiplicity of our individual psyches, transcending any fleeting identifications of the ego, it would seem to encompass who we are in any given moment as well as who we have been and who we will always be.

Reciprocally, through the archetypal ego (or Self as described above), we become more present to the here and now of the image, engaging the image with all our bodily senses—we can smell, feel, hear, taste, and touch the image because of our presence to our own body, Stephen Aizenstat's third attitude. Like what James Hillman described as a revitalization of our sensory awareness, we meet the image from the fully instinctual and highly present sensual self that exists within each of us. Imaginal remembering would require this movement into that animal body that foregrounds the archetypal ego. Being fully open to body awareness may be even more significant given what has been written about by a good many scholars regarding our bodies being conduits of our physical and imagined experiences.[97,98,99]

The fourth and final attitudinal quality of engaging with the dream is to engage the dream in an attitude of not knowing. This perhaps is the most difficult of the four qualities and possibly why we require the other three before we fully embrace the fourth. Our culture certainly struggles with accepting, let alone honoring, the unknown.

> The dream itself is a fact. Everything else is conjecture.
> ~ Stephen Aizenstat[100]

We are hypersensitive to the means as providing us an adequate end, and this is true in many ways of dreamwork (recall our dream snake, and our rush toward meaning that leaves us guessing as to what evil is tempting us in our lives). Yet, it behooves us to be diligently cautious of our bias toward the imaginal that is rooted in the cultural drive toward gaining something of service, especially to our present situation.

In my own practice of working with psychic images, I find there must be an effort made not to force a swift, productive, comfortable, or finite interpretation of the image but rather to allow at least some mystery to remain. Yet, as discussed above, association and amplification feel meaningless if we cannot tie them back to our personal story. So then how does one nourish an attitude of not knowing?

Such an attitude is not a defeated acquiescence to the perspective that no wisdom is to be gained from engaging with the living images of our psyche. Rather, to not know simply means that we foster an acceptance of letting be what is still unknown—what, at least at this point, cannot be ferreted out for a concise and complete answer. Radically, to not know enables us to know more in many ways because we take the image purely and wholly for what it is rather than trying to dissect it bit by bit until it no longer resembles the quite perfect entity that first met us in our dream or reverie. By allowing these images to be just what they are, evidencing their own intrinsic wisdom, we release our culturally developed grip to explain them.

Earlier I mentioned about the first time I had the chance to have one of my dreams tended by Stephen Aizenstat. In my own approach to the dream of stealing into my neighbor's home to find a birthday card that I had intended to send her, I was caught looking only at the act of trespassing: the idea of my dream-ego burglarizing a neighbor was so abhorrent that when I first retold it, I felt shame.

> Images, by satisfying instinct, will in themselves alter the way we live . . . only such changes that are changes in soul can affect the psychic aspect of one's actions and relations.
> ~ James Hillman[101]

When Dr. Aizenstat asked me to approach the dream as a dream, I entered the space by way of the dream-ego, a woman who had some need, some hunger to open the neighbor's metal screen-door, slip her way into the kitchen, and rummage through the mail on the small, round Formica table. Noticing that I was holding my hands at my chest, Dr. Aizenstat encouraged my open body awareness by asking me what I felt in the body: I noted a tug at my heart. Staying present to the dream-images, I found the birthday card and with a swelling in my chest, realized it was my birthday card. By not knowing, not rushing in and exploring what in my life I was shameful of or trespassing on, I found that I was entering a place of rebirth and had two guides. The little black dog was at first the image on the card and then became an enchanting animate, autonomous image of my psyche. The neighbor who was not in the least mad that I entered her home was delighted that I had found my own card, my rebirth, by fully entering the imaginal. Left unknown is the exact reason for my psyche to usher in a rebirth. That mystery nudges me onward.

The challenge comes when we interpret the dream image, doing so because we are trying to conform its intelligence to ours. Rather, in meeting the dream image from a *dulia* perspective, an approach that is in service to the image rather than from an attitude that assumes the image is in service to us, we invite ourselves to fully witness the image. In doing so, we cultivate a relationship with our own deeper selves—we come to experience the image from our intuitive sensibilities, and thus our heart and our soul rather than just our mind.

Further, when we experience these images as real, and engage them as such, we make soul, which is the primary function of psychology according to James Hillman. In making soul, we come to know our own selves, our deepest selves, by recognizing we are but one aspect of the greater universe which stands behind our lives and our lived experiences. Through our open body awareness and our presence to the here and now of the image, the images satisfy the most primordial aspects of ourselves, imparting a deep wisdom that need not necessarily be explained by or to the rational mind because it is making the soul.

Footholds of Imaginal Remembering

Before we turn towards the stories of those who practiced imaginally remembering, I would like to offer anchors, attitudinal and behavioral footholds, that seem relevant to deeply experiencing the living images of our memories. Intuitively, most of these anchors mirror what those who have intimately and carefully worked with the living images of dreams have shared (and have been spoken to already in this chapter). Given the argument that dreams and memories both present as psychic images and might be approached as animate and autonomous from the ego, it stands to reason that what grounds and deepens the experiences in Dream Tending would be similar if not the same in imaginal remembering.

Many of the people with whom I've practiced imaginally remembering also had experienced the practice of Dream Tending and other types of dreamwork. They corroborated similarities between the experiences, including the shared visceral qualities of these practices. Encounters with the living images, whether those images originated from memories or dreams, both involve transformation, where the images autonomy and animation manifest. Julia, whose story is told in Chapter 7, expressed both practices as a "sacred theater" where the dreamer or the rememberer is "reenacting on a deep level," as if the psyche-centered cauldron of these practices invites a new and imaginative approach to what was already experienced.

Indeed, the attitudinal and behavioral footholds I mentioned earlier appear to allow for the existence of this cauldron and its capacity to provide a safe and sacred space for both the living images and the one with whom they engage. The first foothold is the rememberer's willingness to accept and honor the anonymity of the psychic image. This begins even by asking the rememberer which memory seeks to be imaginally remembered (as is similarly done in Dream Tending), where the memories engaged seemed to offer themselves to the rememberers (as shall be illustrated in their stories).

Further, during the practice of imaginal remembering, when the rememberer would begin to speak in past versus present tense, dropping back into seeing the memory versus experiencing the memory as a memory-image, their full and open presence to the memory-image seemed to drift, and they lost touch with the living image. However, most, especially in the deepest and most revealing moments of their tending experience, would use language that expressed their own wonderment and respect for the memory-image and what it had come to reveal.

The second foothold was hinted at by C.G. Jung when he advised that the more one slows down, the more one might fully experience the presence of the memory-image, often in a multitude of sensorial ways (touching, listening, smelling, seeing).[102] When the rush of recollection is softened into a slow, attentive approach, this invites a more available and intimate presence to the memory-image. Further, by being fully present to the living image of the memory, slowing down and allowing for a multisensory experience, one notices objects and figures, details and qualities, not previously heeded. These observations are often fundamental to the experience both in terms of the imaginal remembering journeys and the later reflections upon them.

The third regards the importance of being witnessed. In the imaginal remembering practice, like with Dream Tending, often there is another that holds the cauldron by way of witnessing the rememberer's experience as well as guiding the process (often simply by way of encouraging the rememberer to slow down or to notice what is imagistically or somatically present). For some, this ability to be witnessed, and even more so guided, comes through a level of trust with the one who is holding that safe space.

In Dream Tending, this person is called *the dream-tender*. We might think of them as an imaginal guide, a Sherpa for the imaginal mountains of our psyche. The openness required to fully engage with the imaginal necessitates a vulnerability. Without trust in the imaginal guide, one may struggle to open somatically or psychologically to fullest expression of the imaginal remembering experience. This is important when we acknowledge the idea that our bodies hold these original events and facilitate our remembering of them.[103] It is perhaps even more significant in those cases of a traumatic memory where we must first feel safe before we can feel heard and seen in our re-experiences of traumatic events.[104]

I should note, the process of imaginal remembering doesn't require a guide. You might pick up this book, like the idea, and then enter your own memories imaginally, though it's more difficult to witness oneself as we shall read about in Chapter 5. This approach is a bit more difficult because the mirror as another is a powerful reflection for our own psyche and our approach to our intrapsychic images.

For this reason, it may be nice if you read this book with a friend or trusted colleague and give it a whirl, taking turns guiding the other. The point is that you trust in your guide (to include yourself) so that you may feel comfortable with any vulnerability that might arise. I offer a simple approach to imaginal remembering in the last chapter of this book, summarizing many of these concepts we've been discussing.

The fourth foothold strongly relates to the third and provides stability and support to the first two. If we return to the idea of the Sherpa, this guide of our imaginal mountains, we would want to think of that guide as someone who, himself, believes in the process of imaginal remembering and holds that the images of our psyche are imbued with their own vitality. Furthermore, if we think of those who are witnessing our imaginal experiences (whether through listening to or reading them), we would also want to think of them as holding safe and sacred passage during our journey within the imaginal.

For this reason, I offer this final foothold, a grounding for myself as the writer and a suggestion for the reader. After analyzing and then writing about the imaginal remembering experiences in my early research, I came to recognize that a skeptic might see the participants' descriptions of the phenomena as the willed way of the ego that knowingly or unknowingly created the images shared. Here, you might recall what I said earlier in this chapter: if the images surprise you, you're probably on to something imaginal! This suggests that the ego isn't driving the experience.

Of course, I have no material proof to offer that these individuals did not contrive or manipulate their experiences. To be clear, I do not feel such material proof is necessary or particularly worthwhile. But I will share this story. Robert Johnson described a client who was trying to beat Johnson, his therapist, at what the client saw was the game of active imagination. Johnson wrote of this client.

> You see, even when he was trying to conjure up his "fake" story in order to fool me and ridicule the whole process, that "fake" story had to come out of his own insides, his own psychological "guts" as it were. While he thought he was inventing something, he was spilling out the secret contents of his inner being.... He had tried to fake it. But accidentally, in the process he did his Active Imagination. He experienced the symbols from the unconscious. Finally, his Active Imagination brought him face-to-face with his inner self. He was never quite the same again.[105]

Thus, there can be no "fooling," for whatever is experienced when we engage with the imaginal, is a phenomenological truth simply of itself and meaningful because it is helps us burrow into the deeper parts of our psyches to uncover what lies below. And so now we turn to these truths of the psyche as told by the living images residing therein.

PART II

STORIES OF IMAGINAL REMEMBERING

Is not memory, in short, a royal road to soul?

~ Edward Casey, *Spirit and Soul: Essays in Philosophical Psychology*

CHAPTER 5

REMEMBERING THE LIVED EXPERIENCE OF TRAUMA

The physician and psychoanalyst Dori Laub, who is also the cofounder of the Fortunoff Video Archives for Holocaust Testimonies at Yale University, argued that many survivors (using those of the Holocaust as his example) are terribly burdened by the lack of a witness to their traumatic lived experiences. Given the utter horror of their agonies and the secrecy often surrounding the atrocities suffered, there may be an absence of others to bear witness to them.

However, as Laub explained, the critical witness is not another; rather, it's the self. This self, as the internal witness, holds awareness to its lived experiences within the construct of its held identity. In traumatic circumstances, there is such a deep incapacity "to bear witness to oneself" that "one's identity ceases to exist as well."[106] In other words, one cannot come to reconcile the traumatic experience with its current self. In many cases, this means disassociating from the traumatic event (with no consciousness or inaccurate or spotty consciousness of the event). For example, as a teacher of trauma-informed yoga, several of my students have experienced moments during class when they bear witness to their own physical traumas because they are fully present to their bodies. The practice of yoga harnesses our innate mind-body connection so that these trauma survivors can bear witness to themselves through careful attunement to their soma.

In complement to Dori Laub, professors Bessel van der Kolk and Onno van der Hart helped to make sense of why it is that we struggle to narrate our traumatic lived experiences.[107] They argued that such traumatic experiences are outside of our psychologies—outside the understanding of our current-selves.

There is belief that we do not hold or access these memories in the same way we do those memories that are understood and acceptable. Brain activity involved in remembering the traumatic experience is different than brain activity involved in remembering the typical episodic, autobiographical memory. They suggested it's because a traumatic lived experience is disassociated from emotion, thus it cannot be integrated. In other words, at the point of the traumatic experience, the self becomes frozen and the nonintegrated traumatic lived experience becomes the root cause of pathogenesis (the development of a disorder, be it psychological or physical).

Because the traumatic experience is not integrated, the survivor of the trauma is bound to unintentionally repeat the traumatic experience through lived experiences (such as seeking abusive relationships as either victim or perpetrator). van der Kolk and van der Hart noted that by returning often to the memory of a traumatic lived experience, and by shifting the images of that experience, the survivor can assimilate the experience and thus transform it from trauma memory into narrative memory. These narrative memories, they argued, are not replays of historical events; rather they are a continual mingling of new and old knowledge, where the imagination is actively engaged in order to shift the traumatic memory-image so that healing can occur.

In this chapter, we explore two stories of imaginally remembering the lived experiences of trauma. In the first story, Angeline's, the trauma is explicit. It is a memory of escaping an abusive relationship. In Rasputin's story, the second, the trauma is more insidious. It is a brief memory of a repeated behavior of the young Rasputin, a memory of lived experiences more than 50 years old. The power of imaginal remembering is illustrated in the remarkable ways both individuals moved through and beyond their experiences of engaging with the memory-images.

Saying Goodbye: Angeline's Story

The first time I met Angeline I was struck by her calming presence. A dark-haired and soft-spoken woman, she carries herself with a gentle grace. I had known her for a few years before I first invited her to practice imaginal remembering with me. She knew it was an idea I'd been toying with, and when I asked her about me practicing it with her, she seemed excited but also a little nervous as if she was afraid she wouldn't live up to my expectations. I reassured her, as I do everyone I work with, that there are no expectations to this practice. The imagination is just as it intends to be.

A few months later, I had reason to be in Los Angeles over the weekend, and I offered to drive the few hours distance to where she lived so that we could meet in a comfortable environment for her. Instead, Angeline insisted we meet me in LA, explaining to me that she could make use of the trip beyond just our time together. I was a bit humbled by her willingness to oblige me. She must have awoken early that Saturday morning in January to drive to the hotel where I was staying.

Knowing that we would be meeting at my hotel, I had checked into a room that was a suite with a separate living room area. The room, like many hotels I've stayed, was fairly sterile but plenty accommodating for the work we would be doing together. Later, as I watched Angeline move within our shared physical environment, fully engaged in the imaginal, I wondered if the room's unassuming qualities were an unexpected gift.

The first memory that Angeline felt called to be imaginally remembered was a sweet recollection of the first time she met her love. As it happened, there were two memories that seemed to nag at her, hovering there at the edges of consciousness. For this reason, Angeline asked me for a little more specificity of what type of memory would be best. I offered that she might take a deep breath into the body to see if it might have a suggestion, and, after doing so, she felt the body had provided direction.

She began by telling me the memory of a first date with the man that she, at the time of this writing, is engaged to marry. She explained to me that perhaps the memory came forward because she made "a choice" not to go to the "darker memory." We spoke of the two memories, and it seemed that something was holding Angeline back from working with the "happy memory."

Soon she decided that the "traumatic memory" was more fertile in terms of its "potential to open" because, as she said, "that's more charged, for sure; it gets me in a way." I asked if she felt comfortable talking about that memory. She replied "Oh, yeah . . . that was the one I was going to come with actually." The apprehension to enter in the "traumatic memory" came to be understood in our post-session interview with each other, where we revisited how the imaginal remembering session had impacted her life.

She began by providing the context around the specific memory, noting the adrenaline that coursed through her body as she spoke. She had made the commitment to herself to leave an "abusive relationship" with her fiancé, Allan, some 20 years ago. This was not her first attempt; in the past, such exits had been aborted because of the violence that ensued. Though a therapist had advised her to stay in the relationship for another year or so, Angeline realized that she could not and made the decision to leave. However, she also knew that she needed help and was aided by a psychic who gave her the "very simple instructions of just keeping a political face, taking my time. There was no rush to leave." By going slowly, Angeline created a façade of normalcy for the relationship; to disclose her intention might have led to a violent retaliation by Allan. She described that it was "almost as if this other energy took over where I wouldn't be consciously thinking about it, but I would just be pulling stuff out," removing the possessions of her life from the home she was leaving.

Angeline explained that she lived in a home with Allan and Allan's father, Joe, both of whom at the time of the original event were sleeping in Joe's bedroom because they were quite sick. She shared this memory.

> The night before, I bought some yellow flowers for them. . .
> . And then I knew that I was going to leave the next day.
> God, this is so, so scary to me. Basically, you couldn't really tell that I had a whole lot less clothes there. I had taken a bunch of stuff to the dry cleaners, took stuff back to work, getting a new computer. Let me just get this out of here.

And I hang my clothes up kind of on the hanger. Got dressed for bed, went to bed. Both of them were really sick, so fortunately Allan was in his father's room. I get up at 6:30 in the morning, and I've got the letter ready to go. I leave the letter. We're engaged. I put the ring out, I put that in the envelope, seal it, grabbed my clothes, walked out the door, leave the key, walked out the door, get in my car, and leave in my night clothes. And then I started—it still gets me—I start making phone calls, just to close down, so he can't get to me.

When she had finished sharing the memory, Angeline began to cry, her release of tears coming at the point in the story when she is out of the house, when she has survived the perilous escape. The event itself and the moving beyond it are both traumatic. Survival itself, you see, can be a crisis.[108]

Angeline continued, through her tears, explaining what followed, including specifying that the phone calls she made were to security personnel at the company where she worked so that Allan could not reach her. She also phoned her brother, Adam, because she was heading to his home to meet him and then to "drive up the coast," away from Allan. Within minutes, Allan tried to reach her "incessantly," and Adam kept her from returning the call, since the compulsion to go back was powerful. Of Allan, Angeline described that she was "totally under his control" almost from the beginning of their 5-year relationship because he hardly allowed her access to the outside world, cutting off her relationships with friends and family members. "I didn't have any support."

The relationship with Allan "was a repeat. There is an echo. It happens early in childhood." Allan had been the third relationship in which Angeline had suffered abuse and trauma, where "each time it gets worse." The first relationship was with her father, whom Angeline believed suffered from war-related PTSD. "I was brought up in an environment where no one talked about the verbal abuse, and no one talked about everything that goes on, the kind of tirades that go on." The second abusive relationship, this one with her first husband, ended on the same calendar day (many years prior) that she left Allan. This kind of echo is not uncommon. Rather, this reenactment is the psyche's attempt to resolve the wounds of the past, attempting to heal the emotional scars that trauma leaves behind.[109]

Before we move into the imaginal space of the memory, meeting it as a living image, I asked Angeline where in the body she felt the adrenaline, the sense of hyperarousal, that she noted experiencing when she first began to share the memory. She responded, "It starts in my legs and kind of moves up," where the sensation in her legs coheres with the description of a memory in which she seeks to escape, to make flight, from an abusive relationship.

In fact, Angeline appears to be describing a functioning case of "freezing," the term psychologist and medical-biological physicist Peter Levine used to describe the natural phenomenon of the reptilian brain to render the body and its sensorial experiences immobile.[110] This occurs in order for the victim to go numb to the horrific consequences of suffering from a traumatic event when the other two options of fight and flight are not available. Though humans share this frozen response with other species, unlike other animals, humans do not release the energy of the first attempted fight or flight when coming out of the frozen state. This unreleased energy is what then continues to torment an individual, where the symptoms of trauma are not caused by what triggered the recollection but by this frozen energy that has been left behind, unresolved. This energetic residue of the trauma remains without escape, haunting both the body and the psyche.

Returning to Angeline—once she shared with me the memory as she recalled it, we were ready to enter the memory as an image, ready to invite an animated approach to the memory. I asked Angeline to speak as if it were happening right then—not as a recollection of something that had occurred but rather a re-membering, a putting something together again and possibly anew. Because Angeline was familiar with working with dreams imaginally, she understood the practice of being present to the image and letting it unfold as it may, not forcing it to conform to the ego's intention, or in this case, what is recollected from the past. Yet, Angeline seemed (like others) to enter part way into the memory-image, drifting back and forth in her use of both current and past-tense language. Sometimes she would speak of her surroundings as if they were very present to her, and sometimes as if she was trying to recall what happened in the past. Still, as she spoke, she recognized her body's response, noting "my heart is beating" as she left the memory-image home. I ask her to begin again, staring back in the bedroom before she begins any action that will eventually allow her escape. From here, I will use present tense to help us think about the imaginal remembering session as different from the past.

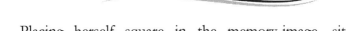

Placing herself square in the memory-image, sitting in the memory-image bedroom, Angeline is "listening really loud" for any sounds down the hall, an odd expression that seems to suggest the intensity of her senses. Listening to their breathing, she is "feeling very scared, very, very scared" and "knowing that I have to act quickly."

Caught between listening and moving, ensuring her safety as well as getting herself to safety, she takes a breath into the body, into the fear, and notes that the breath "feels stuck." Notably, constriction along with hyperarousal and freezing are three of the four elements of trauma—the fourth is disassociation.[111] The groin area, too, is the place of the second chakra and is associated with traumas of sexual and emotional abuse and volatile situations. The constriction felt in this part of the body is self-evident, given the abusive relationship from which Angeline suffers.

With prompting, Angeline looks around the memory-image bedroom to see what, if anything, is drawing her towards it. She notices a "drafting table" in the memory-image that tells her "you are free to go." She leaves the bedroom knowing that nothing is holding her back from going, and finds herself in the hallway "looking down towards Joe's room" where both Joe and Allan are sleeping. At this point, Angeline senses a "real tightness and fear type of clamping down in my groin area. . . . a constriction."

Her body, like the memory-image drafting table, informs Angeline she may go: "You need to go . . . you need to leave this all behind you; you need to let go." Angeline expresses amazement that the "objects" of the home are "witnesses, the house [is a] witness." The memory-image drafting table assures her that it has seen what she has experienced, telling her "I get it." The objects of the home, like her body, held the energy of the abuse she bore. They functioned as her critical witnesses, witnessing her truth of what transpired. In

Angeline's words, "They saw it all." She later explained, "You think that you're not being witnessed or that you are by yourself and that no one else knows what's going on with you . . . the drafting table knew."

Often traumatic events are perceived by the victim as having no witness because the events themselves are so abhorrent it is impermissible to consider that a sane other might be a reference for the atrocities suffered. In Angeline's case, the abusive relationship stripped her of family support, and she, herself, could not bear witness to her incomprehensible suffering.

Angeline is now ready to leave, but then acknowledges her desire to "tell Allan I'm leaving, which is not what happened in the original memory." But here, in the memory-image, that which is influenced by the imagination (and confined by neither the ego nor the past), Angeline states, "I'd like to walk in and tell Allan and Joe that I'm leaving," but, she says in response to herself, it would be "awful to tell them that" because "they're both really sick." She starts to question the desire, noting that "part of me knows better—the logical part"; but some other part of her "wants to just punch Allan in the face and say, 'You jerk, I'm out of here.'" Still, fear holds her back, because "it would be like suicide."

She then notes, in past-tense "I had to get out," stepping out the memory-image, noting what it would have been like at that point in her life were she to have punched Allan as she left. Other memories surface for Angeline, though she does not share them.

I invite her to reenter the memory-image (for it is not uncommon for the ego to pull us away from the imagination), but this time with an ally that can help her stand strong against her abuser, just as Dream Tending[112] and Somatic Experiencing®[113] suggest. Angeline stands up in the middle of the physical room where we hold our session and walks about half way across the floor, stopping and turning toward a blank wall. She stares at it but describes the images in her mind, the hallway and the door of Allan's bedroom. She is in the memory-image, though physically she is standing in a room with me.

Angeline imagines her brother, Adam, there beside her. But the image of Adam in this memory-image hallway is too incongruent with the original event (Allan, she describes, would never have let Adam in the home). The imagination accommodates, and soon the image of her current love, Grant, appears, standing at the far end of the hallway (for Angeline would like to confront Allan on her own). She begins with "just [a] whisper, 'I'm leaving. I'm leaving, yeah,'" noting that it "feels good to whisper because they're still sleeping." I encourage her to say it louder, and she responds, "I think that might wake them up." Still, she continues until she imagistically sees that Allan awakes. Angeline calls out, "No, No, he just jumped up. No." She can now see Grant, who tells her she "can be strong and can do this."

Allan comes after Angeline, but when Grant appears at her side, Allan stops. She notes that Allan is "fading in and out," but she tells him of her unhappiness and how wrong he was to treat her as he did. "Quit haunting me," she cries to Allan, "quit following me. Leave me alone." Facing down the memory-image of Allan, she stares into his eyes, and feels empowered. "I feel like punching…just to punch him right in the jaw." But, she says, "He's not going to stand there." Still, I watch as she swings her fist into the air, and I can only imagine that the punch lands squarely upon the chin of the image-Allan. "He is standing there and letting me punch him" she explains, with the memory-image of Grant smiling encouragingly. Allan is now holding his chin, "glaring at me," Angeline shares, smiling and still staring at that blank wall.

I ask her how her body feels now, and she tells me, it "feels okay," the adrenaline and constriction having been "released some time ago" during her imaginal remembering session. When she decides there is nothing else to do in the memory-image, and it is indeed now time to go, she thanks both Allan and Joe "for meeting me in this place." In return, they thank her for "coming back" to tell them she was leaving. She now feels that something has been completed. "I'm done. We're done. I'm leaving now." Through the imaginal remembering experience, Angeline has re-enacted the traumatic event but chooses a different outcome, this time one that seems to offer the closure that eluded her in the original encounter.

Once Angeline sat back down on the chair, having fully exited the memory-image, I asked her how she felt. She replied, "Empowered . . . to relive that memory in a different way." For most of the remainder of session, Angeline and I discussed ways in which she might continue forward the experience of the imaginal remembering in order that "the haunting stops." She began by explaining that she could "take action" and "not worry about what other people think of my action." Her ability to make her own choices, and voice those choices to others, seem to be joyful byproducts of her sense of empowerment.

One of the most traumatic aspects of this memory is that the escape took place in silence, that there was no real closure for her so that Allan's haunting, through dreams, images, and PTSD symptoms, continued. We acknowledged that in the original event, it was important to leave in silence so that she could get out safely. However, in this case, she said, "it was essential," to say goodbye, "to have it come to a conclusion that way rather than walk out the door without saying anything." She realized then she had said something, but it was by way of a letter, which perhaps did not register for Angeline in the same way that facing Allan and saying goodbye would have.

We continued to discuss ways in which she might solidify the outcome of the experience such that the release of the trauma felt in the body was maintained and the haunting ended. Specifically, I asked her to consider an image of support to confront difficult experiences in her life head-on. She described seeing the image of her father in a photograph. In the photograph, he is standing on a bridge, holding the weight of his body with his arms, hands grasping the rails; his wheelchair is not far behind him, and "he is really smiling."

An odd echo, the supportive image that comes is the image of her father, a man who suffered, Angeline believes, from PTSD and who was the first abuser in Angeline's pattern of abuse. She described that "what the picture says is just to rise above," to "stand strong . . . to look whoever in the eye," facing situations rather than turning away. She also described that her father's image appeared in dreams that seemed to suggest it was time for Angeline to leave her relationship with Allan those many years ago. The beginning, then, aids in ending the pattern of abuse.

Before we closed our session, we spoke of things that would witness Angeline in her life, as the drafting table image did. I asked her, "Is there anything that has energy from the memory-image that seems to say to you, 'Don't forget me?'" Angeline was silent, and then told me, "What was odd was looking in Allan's eyes . . . it was scary. So, don't forget me." She moves on, speaking of the drafting table and other things, but this pause and the recollection of his eyes seemed to be a harbinger of what would come later that day and into her weekend.

When we spoke a little more than two weeks later, Angeline described to me that she nearly experienced another echo of the pattern of trauma and escape. "It really stirred up my whole world. It reactivated the issues . . . on all levels. It's like it reactivated back to the time of the situation of my escape." She noted, "I was re-stimulated with fear for Allan," where she continued to see the image of Allan's "blue eye" that day.

In a strange set of circumstances, Angeline found herself alone that weekend of our imaginal remembering session in a city not her own. She and Grant were apart because he was tending to family business, and, painfully for Angeline, in the company of his ex-wife. She explained, "It actually affected . . . the new relationship that I'm in. I was like, all I want to do is just bail from that . . . and we actually had a little rift." She was "activated from the perspective of fight or flight . . . I was in flight, as in I've got to get away from the current relationship" to the extent that she started to drive away, the same route she and her brother Adam had driven years ago when she escaped from Allan. Before long, she convinced herself not to behave in this way. "I realized that it was the replaying of a pattern." Angeline's case brings up a concern for the process of imaginal remembering; if it stimulates dormant trauma-based energy and imagery, can it be harmful?

It is possible that Angeline's imaginal remembering session was too intense an experience in one setting, where some research suggests that taking it more slowly, over several sessions, may be less jarring and more digestible for the client.[114] The other consideration, though, is that when the pattern arose she was able to witness and choose a different approach, as she expressed hoping to do at the end of our session. In this way, it suggests that imaginal remembering was helpful in assimilating the traumatic events of her escape.

There is another sign that the imaginal remembering session may have been helpful to Angeline. She noted that on the Monday morning that followed our Saturday session, she had the following dream.

I'm in this high-rise . . . and it's really nice. . . .
Everything's just lovely. . . We are 30 or 40 floors in the air
. . . so I'm sitting in this easy chair . . . that's faced against a
wall rather than facing into the room. All of a sudden
there's this massive earthquake . . . I feel a g-force against
my body. It's so intense . . . I know that the building itself
has moved off its foundation like 20 feet . . . my sister . . .
is in the kitchen, and she calls out, "Are you okay,
Angeline?" And I say, "Yeah, I think so," but it was just like
this impact. And then as I get up out of this chair I'm
thinking, "Did I call; did I text Grant?" . . . I wasn't quite
sure if I had done that or not. Then the next scene is I'm in
a spa in the same building [or] hotel. I think it's more of a
hotel than a condo building. And I'm in the spa and this
woman is tending to me, and I'm in my nightgown. And
she looks at me, and she's kind of like doing my nails or
something. And she says, "Oh, you are in your nightgown."
I said, "Yeah, I just didn't feel like getting dressed." And
that was the end of the dream.

Through association and amplification (notably the first time such
techniques are applied given Angeline's session is highly focused on
animation), there are several key symbols of the dream that suggest to
both Angeline and me that the dream is about the imaginal
remembering session and its impact on Angeline.

The first is the context of the dream, a hotel of suites. Angeline
reminded us both that our session took place in a hotel suite that I
was staying at for our work together. She also indicated that the chair
upon which she sat in the dream was very much like the one that she
sat in during most of our time that day.

Second, the earthquake seems to suggest a shockingly
transformative experience. Certainly, Angeline's physical description
of a "g-force" felt in the dream intimates a significant shift, so much
so that a high-rise structure is moved a considerable distance. That
she experiences the earthquake as she faces a wall also suggests that
Angeline was unprepared, facing away, from what the experience
might mean to her. She explained to me, though not in direct
connection to the dream, that "I didn't fully recognize that by talking
about this that I would re-stimulate"; and, at a later point, she noted,

"I think I really did treat the memory too lightly." I would have to acknowledge that I did as well, not realizing the residual impact (not unlike the aftershocks that follow an earthquake) such an experience would have.

That she is turned away when the dream begins might also suggest her past sense of turning away from difficult circumstances, where she explained after the imaginal remembering session that she would like to face such situations directly. To this point, we note that the dream shared with us that Angeline is fine, and her first inclination is to contact Grant.

A "rift" was first experienced in the relationship that left Grant believing Angeline was leaving him and Angeline having felt she "lost the connection to him, the energetic connection that's really important to me in a relationship." Thus, on that next Monday evening, she explained to him the full impact of the imaginal remembering experience, that it re-stimulated her flight response to relationships. Angeline expressed that "communicating the whole thing to Grant was a step in the right direction."

An energetic reconnection was made with Grant as well as a communication, explaining her past tendencies. She explained, "With the tending of the memory, shifting it around, and going in there and doing something different, that will affect how I function, I would think going forward. One would hope." In this way, Angeline faced a difficult situation with Grant and spoke directly to it, suggesting it has already begun to affect how she will approach difficult circumstances in the future.

The dream ends with Angeline in her nightgown (the attire she was wearing when she left Allan). She is receiving "tending" from another, a form of self-care, and when called out that she is in her nightgown, Angeline seems to casually, confidently respond, "Yeah, I just didn't feel like getting dressed." In this statement, we might hear evidence of a woman who chooses "to take action and to not worry about what other people think about my action. . . . I'm going to do what I want to do. I'm happy here whatever the situation is." This is the statement Angeline made immediately following the imaginal remembering session; it was her response to my question of finding ways to ensure an ongoing experience of feeling empowered.

Thus, in closing, we will never truly know how this imaginal remembering session ultimately influenced Angeline and her relationships. There are positive signs to include that she and Grant worked through the difficulty that surfaced after the experience, and later became engaged to one another. She indicated to me in a conversation several months later that the experience itself helped her to communicate with Grant some of her own insecurities about their relationship. However, her story also raises a cautionary note that whenever we are dealing with memories of trauma, it is wise to be hyperaware that our bodies and psyches are intensely impacted by the ghosts of the past.

Being Seen: Rasputin's Story

Though I had spoken once with Rasputin (his chosen pseudonym), on the phone, about his interest in dreams and the psyche, the first time I ever met him in person was on the day of our imaginal remembering session. We met at a hotel near his home, thousands of miles from my own. He had agreed to meet there, finding it to be a better location than his own home or an environment familiar to him. I was waiting in the lobby and seemed to recognize him the moment he walked through the door. Though a man in his 60s, he carries his tall and lanky frame with a youthful, casual stride. His hair is about shoulder length and his eyes are soft and pensive. I offered that we could meet in the hotel's restaurant to have a coffee or tea or something to eat before we went up to the hotel suite, like the one in which I met Angeline, where we would undertake the imaginal remembering session.

I have interviewed a great many people over my years as a research psychologist, so to meet with Rasputin as an otherwise stranger held no peculiarity for me. He was recommended by someone I had complete trust in, so I knew I would be perfectly safe. It had never occurred to me to think that Rasputin himself might feel odd or a little uncertain about me. Here I was, this stranger, asking him to reach into his past, share an intimate detail about it, and then dig even deeper into his psyche and describe to me, perhaps, the truths of his soul.

After about 15 minutes of small talk, I noticed my slight anxiety that we were dilly-dallying away precious moments that could otherwise be applied to imaginal remembering. But then I took in the way he would look at me only briefly before staring into his cup. It occurred to me then that he needed this time, and I did as well. To ask someone to allow you to witness them, well, as I already said, that takes trust, a trust I had not yet earned. So, we lingered there at our little booth in the hotel restaurant, for the better part of an hour, each of us sipping our herbal teas with care and talking mostly about tea and honey. When both our cups were empty, I asked Rasputin if he wanted anything else. He shook his head and said he was ready to head up to the hotel suite. When we arrived, he looked around and selected a chair near the window, and then nodded that he was ready to begin.

Rasputin's is the only memory of its kind in this book; rather than being of a single event, it is a memory of the same repeated event, performed again and again, for what he guessed was the better part of three or maybe four years, somewhere between the ages of four and seven. With astonishing detail, he described the surroundings of an environment intimately familiar to him more than 40 years ago.

It was a sunken living room. As you're standing at the front of the room, it's the far left-hand corner. And there's a small piano. It's an upright. I think it was a Steinway, brown. And it was in the corner, but it was kitty-corner. And the kitty-corner creates a little triangle shape behind it. And so, I would squeeze behind the piano and hang out there. As I was remembering that, I also remember that I used to do it at the house before. . . . The [house that I lived in when] I was seven, [it] has green shag carpeting and wood paneling. [The house where] I'm five has a tile floor . . . the piano's the same. It's the same piano, and on both ends, there're these big wood dowels that are uniquely shaped, and they were for like when you moved the piano, there's like a hold on it. And then there was some kind of hand-marking like in a black ink that meant something to someone. And then I kind of remember some sort of label that is made from pressed metal that gets attached to an object. But I don't remember any words. I think there was a number on it, but I don't remember any words. And so, I would go back there when I was sad or depressed and just hang out. But a couple of times, I would be sad and depressed, and I would purposely go behind the piano to see if anyone really cared that I wasn't even around anymore. And then I remember sitting and being in certain positions behind the piano and hearing people go by, and I would make myself right. I would be like, "You see, no one even notices that I'm not even here." So that's the memory.

The way in which he described the memory seems to foretell the imaginal remembering session; there is a devoid but also quite moving quality in his somber retelling. He later described the house as having a "static" feeling to it, and this makes a fine description for the memory itself. It has little movement; it is unassuming and still.

The memory's composure seems to express the inherent motivation of the teller, to slip into the crevices of the household, to be absorbed by the wood paneling itself, an observer waiting to be observed. Further, he described squeezing himself into a "little triangle shape." J.E. Cirlot shared in his book, *A Dictionary of Symbols*, that the triangle, when amplified, may symbolize an evasion of extension, the desire towards non-extension.[115] As we will see, this is an important amplification given that Rasputin later shares his difficulty with extending himself into the world.

Seeking to understand any personal associations to the memory, why psyche would pull it to Rasputin's consciousness for our session together, I asked him why the memory seemed to wish to be tended. "It's an ongoing challenge for me to be seen" he said, further unpacking the statement and sharing that to be seen is more than just a visual engagement. It takes the person in through all the senses, "sight, sound, being heard, being seen, and seen in the here and now" without projections, without "a preconceived idea of what something means, without agenda." He explained to me, "I have a predisposition to be more comfortable as a background player," no photos, "nondescript cars." This "challenge" as he described it, is "chronic," where nothing had occurred in the recent past that brought it to the forefront, nothing that made it a more relevant topic this particular day.

I asked him a few clarifying questions; each was met with the short, unobtrusive response of "mm-hmm." Yet, when I reached an open-ended question, he politely offered more. I asked him what voices he recognized as he sat behind the piano; the voice of his mother was the only concrete recollection. "I'm sure I heard my dad's voice off in the distance. I'm sure one of my sisters went by, I'm sure. There were pets involved. They didn't find me either." He continued, "I just don't have concrete recall" of any other voices— the vagueness of the people a notable juxtaposition to Rasputin's intimate recollection regarding the details of the small make-shift chamber in which he hid.

I further clarified that the memories were associated to moods of depression and sadness, to which he added, "We could throw in lonely." At this point I asked him what if anything else he wanted to share with me, such as his own bodily sensations. He shared,

> I remember the dirt or the dust on the back of the piano. I remember the cords from the curtains. I think they were green, gold, or whatever curtains. They were kind of pushed into the side next to the piano. I remember feeling bored. It would increase my feelings of depression. How does it feel in my body now? It feels similar to those moments. There's also a little bit of relief. . . . It's safe. It's safe. And like we talked about before, the confirmation of my hypothesis. . . . That no one cares. No one really cares. Not really. And that was a pretty strong theme that I had growing up from a young place. I honestly felt that no one really cared, and I had evidence for that.

Considering Rasputin's answer to my question, it began by first describing the environment. It was dirty or dusty with the drapery cords "pushed" aside—as if to suggest neglect.

I considered what the psychoanalyst Graham Music[116] wrote as I listened to Rasputin. Music indicated that the trauma of childhood neglect and the unfortunate phenomenon that because the neglected child is likely to be so quiet and unassuming, the insidious traumas of neglect go unnoticed and, therefore, untreated. Moreover, even when parents or caregivers take notice of unsettling personality traits, such as the child appearing to be detached if not deadened, and bring the child to therapy, the therapist may have a difficult time addressing the child. Because the child is so empty and inhibited, the therapist must work that much harder to relate in a meaningful way to the child. The therapist's role is to meet the neglected child where he is, empathizing with his emptiness. Once the child/client understands that his emptiness is recognized, even validated, then the therapist can attempt to mirror the child in a way that his parents did not when he was young.

Rasputin's description of the environment then seems to invite self-reflection: a young self who is bored and further depressed but also relieved that he is "safe" and that he is "right" in his hypothesis that no one cares. This notable neglect of the environment in which the young Rasputin hid himself was further dimensionalized as he moved into the imaginal remembering experience. It is as if this outward physical setting, a triangular cell into which Rasputin squeezed himself countless times, mirrored the inner isolated and uncared for young self—a neglected self. Further, this young neglected self appears to still shape who he is today, a man who is, in his own words, "more comfortable as the background player."

The imaginal remembering experience opens by me asking Rasputin to "come back into the memory as though it is here right now." I further invite him to move or to sit but to be present to the memory-images and to describe them to me as he sees them.

> The light wood of the back of the piano, that big hand grip that's made out of wood, the sound board that's on the back side of the piano. On the wall behind me is a rough-cut wood with little slats. They're spaced out every six or eight inches. There's a light and a light chain above me. The light fixture that kind of loops like that. Oh, there's a cord for the light on top of the piano coming down behind. It's kind of musty smelling. Green fabric. Oh, there's a light switch right behind the fabric on the wall. Something kind of curves right here on the right side of there.

Once again, his descriptions are so very detailed and yet so detached. Rather than describe the environment as a space in which he is engaged, he simply speaks, like an outsider, to what he observes of this very intimate, secluded place. He seems to be taking notes of what surrounds him versus living, breathing, and, as a child, developing within those surroundings. He is an object among objects rather than the subject who is in reciprocal engagement with those objects (a phenomenological notion we spoke of in Chapter 4). It's as if the logical details might supplant the vacuum of emotions. Only once does Rasputin stretch beyond engaging with his environment through sight alone. In this case, he notes a "musty smell" that also suggests a space neglect.

He continues, "I'm just sitting in the far section of the triangle. My back's against the wall. My legs are half in front of me, bent. Kind of waiting, kind of bored, kind of looking around." Repeating the language that his back is against the wall (as if this is important), we might hear in the statement the feeling of being pinned back, unable to move or shift of his own free will, "legs . . . bent." We might also intimate from his language a certain "wallflower" persona, a hanging back, a "waiting" for acknowledgment.

Rasputin describes a "kind of grief . . . congestion or restriction" in the chest, where the placement of the feeling is telling. The wounds of the fourth chakra (residing at the thoracic spine or the chest/heart area) are often related to grief, especially as a deficit in our personal relationships.

I ask him to breathe into this space; as he does, he sees an image of a long painting that exists in this childhood living room. The painting, as he describes it, is "long and drippy, and it has like a big thick border, frame around it. It just feels long and dreary. Dreary, dreary's a good word . . . lots of shadow . . . kind of heavy."

He then sees the painting of a young, Spanish girl who he later describes as "stoic, stoic, and stoic, which is a little surprising considering she is relatively young." After experiencing his own emotion of grief, Rasputin sees in these images dreariness and stoicism, suggesting that the imagery itself is a projection of his inner world—an ill-defined and heavy environment that gives way to a child who represses his feelings.

As he looks at the painting of the young Spanish girl, he notes that the house "just feels kind of static, the whole house actually kind of feels static right now. Still, static." Again, the repetitive language suggests the slow articulation characteristic of a neglected child[117]— but also the importance of what is being expressed. If the environment reflects Rasputin's inner self, it is static and lifeless. I ask Rasputin where he feels the stasis in his own body, to which he replies, "In my feet and legs. . . . I don't feel inspired. Yeah, I don't feel inspired to go anywhere, do anything." The deficiencies of the root chakra, which can occur due to childhood neglect, may be experienced as listlessness in the legs, unstable energy that drains from rather than supports the body.[118]

In seeking something that Rasputin can engage, I ask him to touch the parts of the piano that he sees. In doing so, he seems to make a relationship with it, eventually engaging it in conversation. At first, he expresses envy for the piano. "I find it amazing that you get so much attention, because everyone sits down and plays with you. . . . I know you don't get played with whenever you want to be played with, but you do get played."

You see, play is critical to healthy physical development, where playful interactions stimulate hormones that support brain development.[119] The trouble is that when humans (or primates) are reared in isolation, they may never experience play or reciprocally enjoyable interactions. Further, the detrimental effects that lack of play have on a neglected child can lead to the belief that the child (and, later, adult) is an unworthy social partner.

As Rasputin continues to engage with the piano, he hears the piano share, "It's just as lonely for me; yeah it's just as lonely for me. I just sit here waiting." With this understanding, Rasputin comes to see the piano as his "compadre," as if he has found someone who understands him—much like the empathy that is necessary in the therapist-neglected child relationship.

At this point, the imaginal remembering shifts, where Rasputin begins to take some action, first by way of making himself comfortable in his triangular chamber behind the piano, then to commenting that he would like to come from behind the piano and "walk away and not come back." When I suggest to him that he could do just that because this is his memory-image, he tells me he's not allowed, but what he'd like to do is "slam the door." Despite my prompting, no door comes to Rasputin.

He then says, "It feels useless to speak up." When I ask him what he'd say, he responds, "I would want to speak up to my mom and say, 'I'm here, and I matter.'" However, Rasputin cannot see his mom's feet or hear her voice from behind the piano; he responds "no" when I ask if he can call to her.

What he does notice is the memory-image of his father's wheelchair going by. When I ask if he can request of his father to come to him, he tells me, "I don't know if I want to . . . I don't trust her, and she'll use it against me later. I just don't trust her . . . my mom." It would seem Rasputin's engagement with the father is tightly interwoven with the relationship of his mother.

Still, he goes to his father's memory-image, despite the hesitation he feels in his lower body; the piano gives him a modicum of encouragement. He squeezes himself from behind the piano and faces his dad, looking into his eyes. "I see a little sadness in his eyes, too. And a lot of pain. He has more pain than I do. He has more pain than I do," as if finding a connection and a mutual sense of understanding between him and his father. "He wants to say that he's sorry, but he didn't say it yet. . . . I can tell by the way he positions his body." Their eyes drift from each other, and Rasputin notes that he is "wary" to return to a mutual gaze.

As I try to help Rasputin return to the objects of the room for reassurance, he notes that the piano's response is "open-ended," the Spanish girl offers nothing, and the "long dreary" painting is simply there. Though I didn't heed it at the time, Rasputin also notes "a sliding glass door to my back." The memory-image door, earlier requested, has now arrived.

His father is still there, but Rasputin explains, "I don't get the point of having a conversation" with his dad-image "because nothing every really changes." I remind him that this is a memory-image, and he thinks perhaps things could change but then quickly retreats from such "hope." Rasputin, however, tells his father, "It would be good, Frank, if things didn't feel so tight around here all the time." His father agrees but says he "doesn't know any other way." Rasputin then feels the conversation has reached an "impasse." I ask him if he wants to stay in the image, and Rasputin tells me that he "can stay."

I ask him what in the room might help them move through this impasse, and Rasputin finds an odd pineapple lamp to discuss with his dad. This oddity, and the humor that it engenders, opens a door for Rasputin to return to the critical dialogue with his father. "You don't create a safe environment," Rasputin says, further explaining how this is so. His father shifts in his wheelchair and at the same time Rasputin notes his own sensation of "expansiveness."

He continues to describe to his father the hardship of the household's setting but subsequently explains, "It feels like I'm out on a limb. It feels on shaking ground" as if referencing an unstable first chakra. Noticing a tree in the yard, and sensing that he could "take the conversation outside," he crosses through the sliding glass door he spotted before. Out of the home, Rasputin finds a "big tree" with a "big trunk . . . really tall . . . big branches . . . a lot of shade."

He stands against the tree, spine to trunk and sees his father there in the backyard with him. The tree-trunk has been associated to the backbone of the human,[120] where here it seems that Rasputin is leaning against the tree as if to fortify his own metaphoric backbone. Yet, it's not enough, for he remarks, "It sounded like a good idea before. I'm actually going to stand behind the tree now and poke my head around."

With the tree-image providing cover, Rasputin shares again with his father the difficulty of their home life, the punishment he paradoxically receives for both speaking up and remaining silent. I ask him how it feels to express such things to his dad. He shares, "It felt more grounded. Yeah, it felt more grounded, and it felt more like it landed . . . he didn't get mad or blow back, and I'm still standing." We once again hear the language of a first chakra that is perhaps beginning to heal[121]—Rasputin is finding stability and the ability to stand up for himself.

I ask him if there is anything left to tell the tree before he leaves the memory-image. After some silence, Rasputin tells me, "I didn't say anything, but one of the larger branches kind of bends down and kind of strokes my back"—the gentle touch of this tree-image empathizing, validating, and supporting him.

With this, he tells me that he wants to retrieve something from behind the piano, to "come back and get all my unasked-for things so I could take them out with me, so that I don't have to be there anymore." He squeezes back behind the piano and begins to breathe in what he felt he never could request.

I'm just going to breathe them in. When I breathe in, I'm going to ask that it's okay to ask to be comfortable. When I breathe in, I'm going to ask that it's okay to be seen. When I breathe in, I'm going to ask that it's okay to get what I want. I'm going to breathe in [that] it's okay to speak my truth. It's okay to want to see and be seen. It's okay to want to be seen and be seen. It's okay to be seen. It's okay to be heard. And I'm breathing in that it's okay that I'm the one that can go out and create that. I don't have to wait for others. I can do it. And I want to include that I can walk down the street any time I want. Any time I want.

With each mantra, Rasputin takes a deep breath, filling his lungs with a life-force, a sense of self that has not only the right but the worthiness to exist in and among others. It's the breath that animates us, allowing us not only to survive but to thrive by renewing us again and again. Each exhale is an opportunity to let something go, each inhale is a possibility to expand. Through the breath, we gain strength and power as it fuels our cells, clears our minds, opens our hearts.

> The clinical challenge is to stay psychologically alive and hopeful enough to be able to breathe life back into [the neglected child].
> ~ Graham Music[122]

It's as if Rasputin's words are a prayer with a movement towards something, an extension of the self. He begins by first *asking permission for asking for* what he seeks—"I'm going to ask that it's okay to ask." This then moves toward direct permission—"I'm going to ask for...," and then he shifts to "I'm going to breathe in that it's okay to..." He moves to a space of *giving himself* permission—"It's okay to..." His mantra ends with confident demands—"I don't have to . . . I can . . . Anytime I want." Here, his tone is strong, his voice loud. As I write this, I see in my mind's eye an image of Rasputin, his spine straight and long, his feet pressed firmly to the ground, his lungs expanding with each inhale, and an intention of the future carried out into the world on each exhale.

He closes the memory-image with these words, "And this time, I'm going to move the piano so I don't have to squeeze behind it." It is a simple, self-assured statement that requires no repeating, just resolute being.

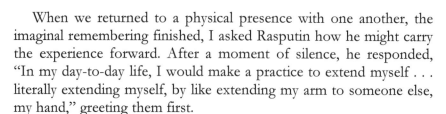

When we returned to a physical presence with one another, the imaginal remembering finished, I asked Rasputin how he might carry the experience forward. After a moment of silence, he responded, "In my day-to-day life, I would make a practice to extend myself . . . literally extending myself, by like extending my arm to someone else, my hand," greeting them first.

If we return to the image of a young Rasputin squeezed behind the piano, pressed against the wall in a triangle container, the image of him extending himself is provocative. Recall that the triangle shape, the shape Rasputin clearly remembers hiding in as a child, is amplified as the desire to elude extension; it is a shape of non-extension. Here then, after he imagistically moved the piano, presumably altering the shape of his cell from triangle to something other, he noted a desire to "extend myself" in the physical world. The shifting of the shape seems to image the desired changes within his psyche and perhaps ego.

He also recognized from the session the importance of having not been played with as a child. "One of the things that I hadn't included before is something really basic, which was just wanting to be played with. . . . I look at that as rather odd that I never considered that, considering it is sort of a baseline for most children." Such lack of play could have created for Rasputin the inability to feel comfortable in social environments, questioning his own agency in such situations.

He continued, "I would be curious as to what else of just really basic needs that weren't being met . . . [that] tried to be met through some sort of unconventional adaptive behavior or something like that." Particularly in this language, we detect the sense of neglect and the way in which the young self learned to cope. To understand these things of the past, Rasputin shared, "would simplify my story." Such simplification might, paradoxically, mean a deeper understanding of why he has become the man he is, why he chooses nondescript cars and wishes not to be photographed. This situation, involving lack of play and basic needs going unmet, would have an impact on how the young Rasputin engaged in the world, learning to approach it from a removed, almost lifeless perspective. That Rasputin still prefers not to be photographed is understandable; he has adapted himself into a person more comfortable not being, in any which way, seen.

We met again a little over two weeks later, this time by phone, and Rasputin shared with me that "for like a day or two, I felt really upbeat and open and empowered." Yet, a few days later, "I kind of hit a wall for like a day . . . went through some sadness and depression. . . . I rebounded in probably a day or so. [The wall] wasn't significant but noticeable." In this very authentic, personal assessment, Rasputin reminded me that to work with one's self, potentially reshaping behaviors so well worn through the practice of repeated patterns, takes time. A onetime experience of imaginal remembering may help us to understand ourselves, and may offer us tools for where to go, but it is not a simple or quick resolution.

He explained to me that he had also been working on the geographical presence he held in his environment, "working with my relationship to walls and corners." When he found himself in a corner or backed up to a wall, he would "sit in the middle of the room or change it in some way." This practice along with giving himself "permission . . . to extend myself" in social situations, had led to the sense of "creating more spaciousness, more inner space around an event, a new way of looking at it."

He shared that an outcome of the imaginal remembering session was "to see some of the underpinnings of that experience in a new and different way so that I'm not bound by them anymore in the old way of perceiving." Particularly, he was re-perceiving himself as someone who would not have to wait behind the metaphoric piano but could reach out into the world, to "be in the flow." Psychotherapy aims to help neglected children eventually reach a place of believing they hold the capacity to actively engage in social interactions, to fully engage with life.[123] In this case, Rasputin was purposefully addressing that in his own personal work. I would suspect that he has been doing such personal work for some time.

In our closing moments, Rasputin told me that the day before, he had been in his childhood home, the one where the original event took place. He had been remodeling the house, an interesting metaphor in its own right. On this particular day, when his remodeling labors had come to a close, he took the time to re-experience the home.

I went into the space, and I actually touched the walls, and the walls are different now because they used to be paneled. I saw the different things that were there, went through a visualization process of seeing the place as it was. And then did things that I didn't do, which was call out and talk to my mom and dad more specifically, that I didn't have the facility or support to do before.

It is as if the adult Rasputin came back to the place of the child to "reclaim," as he shared, something that was left behind. I did not ask him in particular what that was, but it would certainly seem to be a part of himself, that young self, once hidden away, that is finding ways to extend into this world.

Bearing Witness to the Self That Survived

What then do we make of imaginal remembering when it approaches the traumatic memory? Does it hold the power to heal because, as Dori Laub suggested, the rememberer bears witness to the self, especially that incongruent self who suffered the inexplicable trauma? What Angeline's and Rasputin's stories might teach us is that there is something quite moving and healing about bearing witness to the self as it is held in the container of the imagination. In bearing witness to the self, we also might come to understand that we were not alone. The objects of our lives, things with which we, as the subject, are reciprocally engaged, also bear witness to our experiences. Drafting tables and pianos, in the imagination, show us that we are not alone; we never were. Something, even if (all the more if) it is the deepest aspects of ourselves, is there to be present to us, to witness us, through our greatest hardships. When we feel the support of these images, might it be that we can face the darker images of our memory?

What, too, begs acknowledgement is that these individuals, Angeline and Rasputin, who both tentatively entered these sessions, brought with them into the imaginal what seems to me their bravest selves. It strikes me as uncanny that both sought to meet me in an environment quite detached from their own lives. The desire to reach into some of their most profound memories in the sterile surroundings of a hotel suite would appear, from the outside, as counterintuitive. I have invited all my imaginal remembering participants to choose surroundings in which they are most comfortable, in which they feel most safe. And yet the two individuals, whose memories unearth traumas suffered, requested to do their sessions in an otherwise emotionally barren landscape. I trust their intuition had something to do with recognizing the emotionally charged aspects of the memory, and, not wishing to convolute or be convoluted by their sacred spaces, they consciously or unconsciously selected an *elsewhere* for their sessions.

And yet, this hardly kept them from being fully present to the memory-images as they appeared. Both dove headfirst and deeply, each in their own way, exploring what the psyche presumably wished to share. In this way, for the sake of themselves, they were fully present to that traumatized self as it sought to be witnessed in the imaginal.

Angeline would later share with me, as others did, that for me to bear witness to her story was also an important aspect of the process. Perhaps my presence as the guide was the metaphoric mirror that allowed them to reach into themselves and gaze upon the image that exists deep beneath the layers of a person who has learned to cope, learned to survive. What beauty we find when we're able finally to look in the mirror and see our whole selves, scars and all, and claim our lived experiences as our own, whatever they may be. Then to bear witness to ourselves is possibly the most significant psychological work we can do, for in it, we acknowledge that all that has occurred to us, good and bad, has made us the self we are: this one, whom we gaze upon and claim in the mirror of our self-reflections.

CHAPTER 6

SELF-KNOWING, SOUL-MAKING

To understand who I am at this point in my life, I look backward, for in the act of looking backward, remembering, I seek to reconcile my present self with my former self. This looking backward, into the past through the lens of the present, is an instance of what James Hillman described as *psychologizing*, or psychological questioning.[124] It is the agency through which psyche learns and thereby makes soul. We might understand soul-making as the virtue of soul reflecting upon itself through memory, reflecting upon the past self through the eyes of the current self to learn about *itself as the soul.*

These retellings, or re-versionings as Edward Casey called them, may also shift the understood versions of our memories toward something that is *both* personal and archetypal (just like when we observe our psychic images through the methods of personal association *and* transpersonal amplification). Casey described this soul-making reflection as a sort of *active remembering*, arguing that it is every bit as significant to our psychological health as other methods of dreamwork and active imagination.[125] Active remembering purposefully invites the psyche to engage with the rich, transpersonal, a-historical memories of the collective unconscious by seeing them as the backdrops of our own memories. Subsequently, we re-vision or vision our past anew because the memory-images we engage in the process of imaginal remembering are the agents of the soul rather than archives of the physical world. What I mean here is that the soul is both working and worked through our engagement with these memory-images which seek to rekindle the individual soul's connection to the world soul.

Imaginal remembering, then, loosens the *act of remembering* from what is perceived as the rigidity of the past and the physical world, so that we may move *through the depths of the past*, both ours and the collective's, by inviting the self to actively behold itself both in a forward and backward perspective. In this fluid dance of remembrance and imagination, a choreography of past comingled with present and future, the self is known and the soul is made. The memory-images we encounter along the way may also guide us in understanding that each life is not just a solo-act; each of us are dancers within an archetypal ensemble, harmonizing and harmonized with the soul of the world.

In the two imaginal remembering stories shared in this chapter, we snatch glimpses of what appear to be the work of the soul as related to re-witnessing the selves of the past who help us understand and support the selves of the current and perhaps future. Aria's story tells the tale of one who found herself, a paradoxically timid and brave past self, who is most needed and beloved today. In Jennifer's story, we meet a present self who returns to her child self, coming to understand and thus forgive who she once was as well as who she is now. Indeed, Jennifer's story encourages us to witness the mythical underpinnings in all our lives.

The Self Forgotten and Found: Aria's Story

I can clearly remember the first time I met Aria. Both of us were attending a workshop related to dreams and the psyche. I recall the way she laughed, her blond curly hair bouncing about her shoulders. A pleasant chuckle, it seems to express genuine amusement with the humorous situation and with herself as experiencing it. I came to realize Aria is the kind of person who can stand the middle of psyche's river, deeply awash in the current of the imaginal, without ever losing her grounding to the physical world.

Aria has been interested in dreams since the age of six, when she began to journal them. She described her work with dreams as "spiritual, a spirituality connected to myself. I found them supportive when my external world was unsupportive—when it was challenging." She described hearing, many years later, a quote from Jung that she shared as "'dreams are an unopened letter from God.' It resonated because that's how I'd felt about them."

We agreed to meet for our session in a mutual friend's carriage home not far from where Aria lived. The home is situated on the side of a mountain, where the big picture windows seem to recognize the resplendent view of the tall evergreens that, this weekend, had been brushed with fluffy white snow. I felt as though the windows smiled along with me as I gazed through them, soaking in the beauty of the outside world.

Aria and I settled into this beautiful space one Sunday afternoon; she took a seat upon the sofa and me on a chair that cock-eyed faced her. She began by sharing that she did not yet know which memory she would tend. Although I met others who were undecided about which memory to engage, only Aria seemed to come without even a hint. She asked me if I would be giving guidance, and I suggested the memory would be the one that seemed to be called by the psyche. Her response was "I think that's been my approach; I have just been open and nothing. . . . I'll keep my eyes open."

We took a moment of meditation, something I had begun to do after my first several practices of imaginal remembering. During the moment of quiet, an image of a home appeared to Aria, one in which she lived briefly more than 25 years ago. Rather than a specific memory of an original event, the memory was more of a place, a container so to speak, where major shifts in her life occurred. Aria's attention to a space rather than a specific event relates to the significance of place in those memories that shape our selfhood.[126] She shared with me this recollection.

I found myself in a house that Marcus and I had built. I had to be right around thirty-one, thirty-two because the interesting thing about that house was that we lived in it for a very short time. We went through the process of having it built, and doing all the choices, and picking, and all that kind of stuff. We only technically lived in it [about] seven

months before we got transferred. Being in that house, the
memory I went back to was of a time in my life that I was
very much wrung out. . . . There was a lot of transition that
happened in me in that house, even though it was such a
short period of time.

She continued by describing that in this home, she signed up for her
first college course, a psychology class. This was a significant
undertaking for Aria, who would later share that she didn't have
much belief in herself as a student (a woman who now practices as a
doctor of clinical psychology).

She also described her first day of class in which she felt very
excited that "I had raised my hand and shared. I still [was] kind of
shaky as I was leaving and very exposed." She remembered, when
leaving class, tripping over a concrete parking divider, ripping her
new jeans, and bloodying her leg. When she got home, she shared her
evening with Marcus, her husband. "I'm like crying and trying to tell
him what happened, and was like, 'but I shared and then I fell
down.'"

She continued, "But just realizing how much courage it took and
how I'd lived in that house for such a short period of time. It was
almost metaphoric in that way . . . like I had certain things I was
supposed to accomplish during that time, and it happened so fast."

Living in this home was where "an adventure started." The
dreams she had in the home seemed to, through association and
amplification, symbolize what materialized in her physical world.
There were "dreams of swimming across the river from west to east.
And then moving to the east and going from that one class to going
full time, and the rest was history." The river can be an archetypal
symbol of a vital fluidity and a promised rebirth.[127]

Because Aria offered memories of several original events, I asked
her where the memory seemed to open.

The kitchen family room area. . . . I would sit at that
[kitchen] table and write dreams for hours, and work on
them for hours, and do rituals, and fairytale work, and
flower essences, and herbal stuff. I mean, it was just the
place. . . . I started right in that kitchen.

The kitchen has been portrayed in fairytales and myths as a magic cauldron because it is a space where not only foodstuff transforms into that which nourishes us physically, it symbolizes the development of the self where our lived experiences nourish the transformation of our psyches. As Aria spoke of it in her memory, and (as we shall soon see) engaged with its image, the house, specifically the kitchen, seemed to provide the alchemical container of her own rebirth.

Aria begins the imaginal remembering experience by describing to me what she sees as if she is a movie patron, observing rather than participating. When she has finished, I ask her to stay for a minute in the kitchen, looking around it, noticing anything that comes alive, beckoning her attention, even her touch.

With this, Aria recalls another memory, the image vivid, of wild pheasants she is preparing for dinner. She sees the pheasants on the counter with "a big cutting board"; she is "prepping them." As she works with them, she notices that "I've never done it before, and I feel totally at ease. Sort of, 'Oh, I got this.'" This preparation of food can be a metaphor for the preparation of the self, where "the kitchen represents a container in which diverse ingredients undergo processes of chaos and order, merging and separation, heating, cooling, decoction, distillation, and transmutation." [128]

Recognizing her own creativity in the kitchen, she depicts the "sweet and savory" mix of the side dishes she is preparing, and the palpable energy of the family who is excited for the meal. It is a "special dinner kind of energy"; with this, she recalls how much she enjoyed "making dinner . . . feeding . . . taking care of [my family], being a mom."

Aria admits that though this self is "well-suited for this job," she feels "in my solar plexus" the fear experienced by her younger self. The solar plexus approximates the location of the third chakra, the chakra associated to discovering our ego-identity; it is the image of the burning fire that empowers us, wills us, toward our own true self. [129]

Aria continues, acknowledging that "the younger me is nervous. She's really comfortable in the kitchen. Yeah. She could just stay here. She's thinking about it, but she knows she can't stay in the kitchen either." Something seems to will her beyond.

I encourage Aria to continue to feel her way around the memory-image. She is pulled to something "over by the table . . . a spiral notebook . . . [of] flowers . . . plants or herbs, something that she is studying." Aria is in "awe of it," questioning how "it got started." The spiral notebook-image explains that it came from "her, the young woman." It is at this point Aria enters into a direct dialogue with her younger self, no longer as an observer but as an active participant in the memory-image.

Her younger self describes to Aria that the study began "when her husband got really sick [and] almost died." Younger Aria shares her intense enthusiasm for this study, which both inspires and also scares her. Aria remarks that because of her studies, there are "people showing up in her life for help," recognizing that her younger self "knows what she is talking about." She keeps track of her studies in these spiral notebooks, "afraid she'll forget. . . . Sometimes they are questions, sometimes they're insights." Aria, in our final interview, shared with me her recollection that these sketchbooks were lost in the move from this house—it's as if they've been reclaimed in this imaginal remembering session.

As Aria speaks of these studies, she's caught by the rosemary that's on the counter with the pheasants, and then she is drawn back to the sketchbook. There she finds a "two part [sketched] image" of both "rosemary" and something else; "behind it is called a forget-me-not." While forget-me-nots evidence in their name the request of the giver to be remembered, what Aria doesn't consciously realize is that oil from rosemary is used to improve memory-loss. The younger-elf is focused on the rosemary but also tells Aria that the "forget-me-nots are really important."

As she runs her fingers over the sketch paper, Aria recalls how the forget-me-nots feel, with the "silky, velvety" quality of their leaves. I ask her where the rosemary is now, and she replies, "Not far away," noticing that the memory-image has shifted to her grandmother's homestead, where both a large rosemary bush and forget-me-nots bloom from the seeds she scattered long ago. She sits beneath a tree, there feeling both the warmth of the air and the coolness of the earth below.

Myths in which humans are transformed into trees describe tales of entanglement, fixation, and also endurance. Alchemists believed that "the tree may represent not only a place of awakening to new life, but also a suffering . . . of sacrifice."[130] As Aria sits beneath the tree and feels "connected here," she notes, in a tone of surprise, that her younger self "was a long way away." This younger self "has things she wants to do. . . . She's anxious to go on that adventure, she's inspired." To sit beneath the tree in this "sweet place" is "not really what she wants to do." Aria then feels torn as she notices that though she enjoys the respite, she too is "stuck here" in this place on her grandmother's land.

She wants to join this younger self on an adventure, but then she realizes she already has. On a trip to Italy, where the memory-image has now shifted, she understands, as she recalls the images of that trip, that this younger self was also present. It's as if Aria is now seeing the trip again, but through the eyes of the younger Aria.

In the imaginal remembering session, Aria disembarks off a boat (something she did not do in the original event), and is led, though feeling "chilled" and "scared," through the narrow streets of this little Italian town. This time, it is Aria's younger self who is confident, "staying just ahead of me . . . excited." As she follows the younger self, she notices the beauty of what is around her, including a single red geranium. As an emblem of seeding-places hidden within ourselves,[131] the flower here seems to represent the psyche's encouragement of rebirth, beginning with the seedling of the younger self already within Aria.

She follows this younger self eventually into an "everyday" kind of chapel, though it is notably "ornate." The chapel, and its pews, are well worn from their daily use; "they [have been] used for a long time; long, long time." She notices in this space that "the spirit's really present here" though it is called by "ordinary things . . . human" things.

In response to Aria's question, the younger self replies that she has brought Aria to the chapel because Aria "forgot . . . forgot that it's fun." From this younger self, Aria seeks her "energy, enthusiasm, spark" and the younger self seeks Aria's "wisdom and confidence," acknowledging "I don't have anybody like you." They agree to meet here, in this chapel, feeling "supported by something bigger than both of us," and seem to consummate this reunion by lighting little candles in a "blessing of gratitude for each other."

Symbolically, the candle is associated with consciousness, and it illustrates the sustained glow of the sacred and divine as well as our own hopes and dreams. When we light candles in places of worship, we are taking part the act of suffusing the divine into the ordinary world including that introspective flame within in us that guides our path towards self-understanding.[132]

The imaginal remembering session ends here, as Aria, on her own accord, comes into quiet contemplation. It is as if this closing image, the two selves joined together by candles glowing in this sacred space, intimates Aria's return to herself, perhaps even the higher self, as the wise, internal guide whom she seeks.

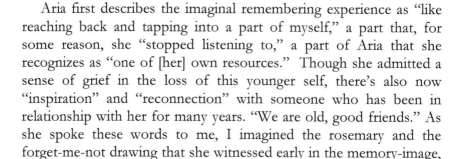

Aria first describes the imaginal remembering experience as "like reaching back and tapping into a part of myself," a part that, for some reason, she "stopped listening to," a part of Aria that she recognizes as "one of [her] own resources." Though she admitted a sense of grief in the loss of this younger self, there's also now "inspiration" and "reconnection" with someone who has been in relationship with her for many years. "We are old, good friends." As she spoke these words to me, I imagined the rosemary and the forget-me-not drawing that she witnessed early in the memory-image, images that beckoned a remembering.

When I asked her the reason that perhaps this memory-image came to her, she recalled that it was of a time "after my husband had just gotten back on his feet after being sick for like 22 months and almost dying." In this time, she "discovered all these alternative forms of medicine" for herself, but also because the "medical profession" had told Aria and her husband that "there's nothing we can do for" him.

The phase of imminent death had passed, but Aria now felt "stuck" that life wasn't moving forward. She also admitted that she "had come to believe that I wasn't smart," receiving such messages from her family. This remembered time in her life was a tremendous moment of moving forward, of rebirth, to a new understanding of herself as an intelligent woman. Such renewed perspective on herself began with the intellect and intuitiveness of studying the healing properties of the plants and helping others better understand themselves through dreamwork.

Guided by the technique of association, I asked her what now in her life might be bringing such imagery forward. She began by explaining to me that "there's some confusion now, confusion with my relationships." Aria noted that she's "always worked so hard to stay connected [with people in her life] for fear I'd be pushed aside." Too, she recently had undergone another life-death experience, this time nearly losing one of her parents. She admitted, "I'm so tired of all the chaotic drama that I absolutely have to stop and do something for myself, but I don't know what the consequences will be." For Aria, this sense of taking time for the self exists in direct conflict with staying connected with others, for to be present to herself means potentially to be out of presence with others in her life. However, she received from her younger self this question—"What if we just have each other?"

This notion of being present to the younger self was exciting for Aria, who admitted to having "so much appreciation for her," a person who had the courage to be reborn, rewriting her life from the old story that she wasn't intelligent enough to be a college student, let alone the doctor of psychology she is now.

We spoke more about the focus of the memory-image on just her own self, where the younger Aria was the only human image who appeared. This reminded Aria that when she was six, she had an important dream that functioned, to some extent, as her initiation into the dream world, not only "on a literal level but on a spiritual level." In the dream, Aria sees a woman who, in the physical realm, has taken her own life; she says to Aria, "You're going to have to be stronger than me. I couldn't do it."

Aria shared, "There's been times in my life around death [when there is a] rebirth that happens." The imaginal remembering session, in the context of patterns in her life around death and rebirth (as the river image foretold), suggested that Aria is coming into another stage of rebirth, and this time her younger self is her "ally" in part because she has made it through such circumstances.

We discussed how the younger self will have a potential impact on the future self as the younger and current selves commune with each other. She explained to me that by moving slowly in the memory-image, she was present "not just [to] witness [the younger self] or observe her, [but] just be with her . . . to be in connection with myself." She stated, "I loved having permission to just go back and collect her." So here again, Aria spoke of "connecting," but this time it is a connection to the younger Aria, a connection that is "loved" and permitted. She has reclaimed a valuable piece of her entire self as the image of the flower, the red geranium, seemed to symbolically suggest.

When Aria and I met for our final phone conversation about two weeks after the imaginal remembering session, she told me that the connection with her younger self had deepened, in part because she has been taking the time to be in quiet meditation with the image of her current and younger selves in the chapel holding hands. This younger self has also been examining the current circumstances of their life, primarily the relationships with those she loves and for whom she has physically cared.

The younger self, Aria noted, has been bewildered by the current existence of old relationships. For Aria, this helped explain her own current sadness about these relationships, and how she's come to give up so much of herself for them. Aria acknowledged that together, she and her younger self have been "very conscious about where we go from here in the future and the present. . . . She is somewhat of a muse for me . . . but also, she's the one that did the work that got me on the right path" in finding her calling as a psychologist.

Since our time together, Aria also recognized that this younger self may have been trying to push through to her for at least several months. Aria noted the synchronicity of a song she first heard at a pivotal point several months ago, a song that feels like a calling from the younger self to be remembered. She also noted a dream that arose about the same time. In the dream, she leaves her beloved dog, Buster, in the basement for days because she forgot him. When she lets him out, she feels remorse. Buster wishes to go explore the woods, but Aria is fearful he will be harmed. She then realizes he has the intuitive, instinctual, and adventurous sense to navigate these dark woods.

As we explored in Chapter 4, the dog may archetypally symbolize the psychopomp that guides us between life and death as well as death and rebirth. The dog, too, "can find what we have lost in the proverbial woods of the unknown."[133] Indeed! The dream seems to suggest that Aria's instinctual self is seeking, and will eventually find, that reconnection with her younger self who wishes to and will aid in this coming transition of death to rebirth.

The Child Who Runs and Remains: Jennifer's Story

I met Jennifer one autumn at a retreat in the mountains. Even though she was new to the space, she carried herself as if she were right where she was supposed to be. It had an odd effect on me, since I had spent the first evening feeling a little lost, a little bit like an outsider. Soothing my own insecurities, I suppose, I tried to get to know Jennifer but found my experience of her was simultaneously friendly and aloof, something that caught me off guard since she seemed so confident. As the days of the retreat wore on, the armor she wore—which I came to see as both what made her shine as well as what protected her—began to peel away, layer by layer. Those of us who did not know her well began to experience a different woman than the one we'd met that first night sitting around a glowing fire.

We met again a year later at the same annual retreat. She greeted me as though she had no recollection of our encounter the year before, welcoming me like I'd never come to the retreat (though I'd been more times than her). I found it a little painful since so much deep and personal material is shared during our time together. Then one morning, I offered to take a photo of her sitting in a rocker on the porch of the meeting house, suggesting to her how beautiful and peaceful she looked there alone in the chill of the morning air, staring out onto the snowcapped mountaintops. She smiled and accepted my offer, and at that point, seemed to also accept me. Several months later, I asked Jennifer if she'd be interested in working with me as I explored the subject of imaginal remembering. She was more hesitant than others but agreed, meeting our work together with the same intensity that I'd seen her bring to the personal journeys of these retreats.

I phoned her late one morning to explain what we'd be doing when we met in person about a month later to practice imaginal remembering. It was during this call that a memory "popped in" to Jennifer's mind. She had acknowledged its presence but wanted to stay open to others. Since nothing else had surfaced over the month between the call and our session, Jennifer shared with me, in the same lovely carriage home where I'd worked with Aria, her very precise, concise memory of an original event some fifty years ago.

> I'm not sure how old I am, I'm probably in the neighborhood of ten, eleven, nine . . . My sister, my dad, and I are in Big Basin in the Santa Cruz Mountains. It's either a state park or a national park, I can't remember. It's the huge tall redwoods, huge trees, and we are just leaving a fireside program with the ranger. . . . It's very dark outside. So, we're walking back to the pickup truck, and for some reason, which I don't remember, I am really angry at my father. We're supposed to be getting in the truck, and I'm on the passenger's side, and I'm so angry that I walk off. I follow the rest of the flow of the people from the campfire who have flashlights, which I don't have. Everyone's walking back to the camp, and I'm following along. . . . The moon must have been fairly bright . . . I walked all the way back to our campsite. I have pretty good sense of direction, so I could find our campsite. I proceeded to sit on the picnic bench and waited for my sister and my dad to show up. He, of course, didn't know where I was, had no idea. So, he'd gone to the rangers, and they were out searching for me, and at some point, I guess they decided to come back and check the campsite because Dad came back . . . and found me sitting there waiting for them. That's when I found out all the rangers were out looking for me because he had to go back and tell them to call off the search because I was sitting on the picnic bench waiting for them. I don't remember him being angry with me. I think he was just so relieved that I was there and safe.

We began by clarifying the background that Jennifer had referenced before sharing the memory. Her parents were divorced at this point in her childhood. The pattern of "If I get pissed off, I'll take off. Or if I'm angry, I may or may not communicate, I'll just disappear" had been present with her since early childhood. She recalled a similar event she believed occurred before the event of this memory, when she left without telling anyone where she was going.

She still practices that behavior in her life—"the pattern just happened last Sunday," she told me that snowy afternoon we met. During these disappearances, just like in the memory she shared, she always held the sense that things will "resolve, if only that we don't get back together again. I don't always know where I'm going because I'll take off, and I'll figure out where I'm going then." She rationalizes this behavior—"My mom raised me to be self-reliant, so it's like, 'I can take care of myself,' and it's like 'I don't care.'" Jennifer's sense of confidence, though, is coupled with a desire to understand this urge to leave when anger arises. She was "curious" about the memory both "because it was never mentioned again in the family" and because "anger's also a good thing to always investigate." It's as if Jennifer is seeking to better understand who she is now, in part, by going back to her very young self.

Before we began the practice of imaginal remembering, I asked Jennifer if the memory still felt alive since it had "popped" into her head a month ago. She responded, "I can remember walking in the road in the forest and the trees." This vivid presence of the natural surroundings and the brightness of the moon in her memory are not only significant to the imaginal remembering experience (as we shall soon see), but they also suggest an emerging archetypal theme that is well-illustrated in the Greek goddess Artemis.

Artemis is associated with pre-adolescence as well as the wilderness, both a time and a place where we experience solitude.[134] Often depicted in a forest setting, Artemis envisages divine femininity mirrored in a nature imbued with the freedom of a wild, brilliant, and unapologetic purity; simultaneously tender and hard, kind and cruel.[135] In Artemis, we see that nature fosters the dichotomous reality that discord resides with sympathy; a rush of movement exists alongside rest. Artemis portrays the archetypal tendency toward disappearance and remoteness, illustrating the autonomous traits of nature to which she belongs. In Jennifer's desire to be more deeply introspective, her experience draws forth the archetypal drive of freedom that is born in and of the ability to find contentedness in the company of only one's self.

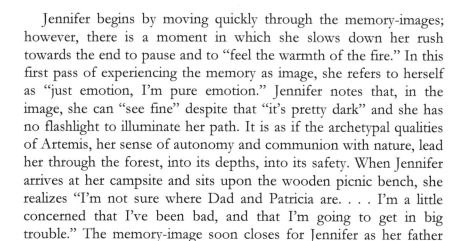

Jennifer begins by moving quickly through the memory-images; however, there is a moment in which she slows down her rush towards the end to pause and to "feel the warmth of the fire." In this first pass of experiencing the memory as image, she refers to herself as "just emotion, I'm pure emotion." Jennifer notes that, in the image, she can "see fine" despite that "it's pretty dark" and she has no flashlight to illuminate her path. It is as if the archetypal qualities of Artemis, her sense of autonomy and communion with nature, lead her through the forest, into its depths, into its safety. When Jennifer arrives at her campsite and sits upon the wooden picnic bench, she realizes "I'm not sure where Dad and Patricia are. . . . I'm a little concerned that I've been bad, and that I'm going to get in big trouble." The memory-image soon closes for Jennifer as her father and sister arrive at the camp, and he sees her and leaves to tell the rangers that she's been found.

Because it's the one image that begs for her attention despite her rush, I ask Jennifer to return to the memory-image of the fire, staying very present to it and noting her feelings. She describes herself as feeling happy here—"I just love the trees; the whole place is magical . . . the air is fresh and crisp . . . it's a beautiful place, and it's out of the city, and I'm with my dad." When we stay at the fire, Jennifer feels happy; but as the ranger's presentation ends and people begin to move, her mood shifts. "I must be talking with Dad because, at some point in there, that's where I get angry."

I ask her to not yet come to the truck, the place in the memory from which she flees. We stay at the fire, and she feels its warmth becoming a sense of warmth and fullness in her own physical body. She also notes the pleasure of being there with her father, whom she eventually, in the memory-image, reaches out to embrace, and finds that he hugs her in return. The embrace feels "warm and affectionate, and comforting and solid." She tearfully shares, "I miss him a lot that he's not there, so perhaps I am a little clingy. . . . I don't want to let go. I'm attached."

With this, Jennifer seems to rise up from the memory-image, like a dolphin coming up for air. She describes, now in past tense, how much she loved, even "favored," her father. When I ask her to tell the memory-image of her father how she feels, she states, "He laughed. Then he would proceed to tell me that he loves all his children," her language shifting from the present memory-image to the past of her lived experiences. Her father, she explains, had two other children, Jennifer's half-brothers, who weren't born before this memory's original event occurred. Her stepmother, though, "would have been around even if they weren't married because my dad left for her." Her language intimates that she views her father's leaving as not just an abandonment of her mother, but of herself, as well.

Jennifer reenters the memory-image at the point in which people are leaving the ranger's presentation, and returning to their campsites. She heads toward her father's truck, but his presence is somewhat uncertain, though she believes Patricia is at her side. Her body is now feeling "a little agitated," sensed first in the legs but then as "energy rising up in my chest. I'm getting anxious or agitated." The surrounding of the warm fire has shifted to the sounds of car doors slamming and headlights beaming. These new sensations "break the spell . . . break the elemental fire and the forest" in their "intrusive, mechanical" ways. The warmth in Jennifer's chest mutates to a "roiling black cloud" and a feeling that she's "helpless."

Jennifer describes being "clingy" to the memory-image of her father, and, in the original event, "he left" Jennifer for her stepmother. I am reminded of Anodea Judith's work on the chakras, where, "Trust or mistrust is a basic element of your first chakra program, which is the foundation for all the other programs that follow."[136] The first chakra is also fundamental to the healthy function of all other chakras. Referred to as the *muladhara*, it is associated to our parents, to our survival, and thus to the first experiences of our self. When there is fear of neglect, there is a corresponding reaction of helplessness, as sense of feeling ungrounded. During these developmental years, the experience of abandonment may result in an excessive first chakra which is evidenced as hyper-fixation on security, food, and attention from loved ones. The things that seem to fill or ground us.

This sense of abandonment surely would have been traumatic for the young Jennifer. The agitation and anxiety felt in the legs during the imaginal remembering experience correspond to a sense of feeling on shaky ground, or perhaps that there is no ground (or grounding) at all. These are aspects of a first chakra that are dysfunctional, where the sense of foundation that is created by a stable home environment is absent in these younger years for Jennifer.

I ask Jennifer what in the memory-image might give her strength. She quickly notices the trees nearby, describing them as "huge," with "fibrous" bark; "in the darkness, they're outlined by the stars." In the presence of the trees, the black cloud is forgotten, but then re-experienced as "sadness . . . the fact that my parents aren't together, a lot of sadness about that." In seeking guidance from the trees regarding her parents' divorce, she understands that "These trees have lived for thousands of years, and the stars have been there forever." She shares, "I feel really small, like it's not significant. The world is just so huge and amazing, and I feel like it doesn't really matter." Though she describes herself as small, it does not appear to be a self-denigrating comment; rather, she seems to be placing her own situation within the greater context of nature as an archetypal experience.

> Any human being is rendered small and young by a great forest, seemingly endless and eternal.
> ~ Ami Ronnberg[137]

She stands in awe of the trees, seeing them as "magnificent" and noticing "a heartbeat . . . a vibration, a rhythm" that seems to manifest from them. In this way, she is feeling the life of the trees and the forest itself. In this place, though she is "all by myself in the forest . . . on my own" she is "confident." Stopping here in the forest, in the darkness, she awaits the dawn's light so that she can see and move again. Alone in the blackness, she still "feel[s] protected in some level. I don't know. I don't think anyone is going to come hurt me. I'm not really afraid of the animals." Perhaps the protection Jennifer feels is the primordial connection to nature in both its darkness and light, as illustrated in the goddess Artemis.

As she sits there in the woods, she expresses a longing for her parents to "get back together, for it to go back to the way it was." She has walked into these woods alone, to be here by herself, because "I don't trust people not to leave. I need to be self-reliant." Seen another way, perhaps this young Jennifer escapes from the human relationship with her father to find, in that solitude, the ability to reflect upon herself and her loss, gathering from the trees and the stars the exquisite impermanence of her current circumstances. "The trees just say you endure. . . . You go on, and you just trust life, you just

> Artemis personifies a force which urges us to withdraw from human relationships and to seek elsewhere, in solitude, another kind of self-realization.
> ~ Ginette Paris[138]

keep going. . . . You keep doing what you need to do, and not everybody makes it." In this language, I recall her confession that when she leaves relationships, she believes things will "resolve, if only that we don't get back together again." There is an accepted loss in living for Jennifer, awareness that compassion lives alongside cruelty, just as Artemis personifies.

The dawn eventually comes, and she sees a mother deer and her fawn. She expresses the "greediness" of the doe that stands in a small, fenced clearing and is handfed grain by campers. "What's occurring to me," she says, "is that it's detrimental" for the doe to eat such grain, where the doe "shouldn't be depending on the tourist to feed" her. It is an intriguing reflection not only regarding humans' interference with nature, but also on Jennifer's own relationship with food—she later notes a frustrating fluctuation of her own weight and a general desire to be thinner.

Recalling the first chakra, when there is damage to the root system of the developing human due to abandonment, the compensating behavior may be to overeat, as if to fill the body with some false form of stability.[139] The wise image of the doe and her dependency on the tourist may reflect Jennifer's internal knowing that she cannot rely on food to fill the gaps left behind in childhood. It may also reflect her desire and subsequent behavior to never be dependent upon another for her own sustenance, something Jennifer has also expressed.

In the memory-image, her father and sister have now joined Jennifer, and she realizes the value of their presence (along with an appreciation for her friends and her mother who have also joined her in the memory-image though they weren't there in the original event). She knows "that I'm strong and that I can take care of myself," yet she also recognizes, "I love them," and knowing this makes "me stronger."

She hugs her sister, acknowledging their "unconditional love" for one another. She tells her father that she will "always . . . be daddy's little girl, and I know you did the best you could." Still, she expresses sadness that even in the memory-image, he seems "distracted," and she cannot hold his gaze. The memory-image shifts to a final image of the day she asked her father not to pass from this world without saying goodbye to her. As she tells me this, she is softly crying, and she once again exits the memory-image.

I ask her if there's anything left that she needs to understand about the memory. She responds, with the image of her "walking away from the truck" arising in her mind's eye, "There is an unanswerable question of why I, sometimes, turn my back on people that love me." Jennifer's behavior is understandable when considering that abandonment occurring in childhood can resurface as a hypersensitivity to abandonment in our adult relationships, where we may too quickly interpret others' changes in mood or slightest criticisms as evidence of their ensuing abandonment. In Jennifer's case, she appears to respond to such fear of abandonment through the mechanism of escape.

She agrees to come back to the memory-image and walk away from the truck. Doing so makes her feel "energized . . . really determined, strong, purposeful, and willful," as if she's buttressed by the anger (born of fear) that drives her to walk away. She describes that the anger "is powerful and can motivate me, but it's not sustainable." I ask Jennifer to keep walking willfully, and to notice what happens. She expresses that "the energy is going out of my feet, it just drains out." Again, Jennifer's language speaks to her sense of a depleted foundation; there is nothing to sustain the energy of her determination.

I ask her to return to the memory-image, this time walking from the truck, and to feel sensations of willfulness, confidence, and anger, but I counsel her to stop as soon as she feels her energy start to drain. Upon doing so, she indicates, "I feel rooted like a tree. . . . I don't feel anger. I just feel strong. . . . I'm standing up really tall and straight . . . my shoulders are back, my head's up, and I can look at the sky." It is the feeling of being "powerful . . . that if I'm determined, and I stick with it, it'll happen." Jennifer finds power and determination as an image of a tree, rooted to the earth, firmly grounded.

We see again the relationship to Artemis in Jennifer's love of Earth Mother—it is Earth and nature that provide her the solid foundation that her own parents could not. Too, the image of the tree is a symbol that we must grow downward if we are to grow upwards, with roots reaching deep into the earth that stabilize the trunk so that the limbs may rise to the heavens. Though the first chakra may have been damaged by the initial wound of childhood abandonment, the archetypal image of Artemis exemplifies finding fortitude within self and nature. Rather than seeing her "walking away" simply due to defiance born of anger, we now envisage the departure as a way of seeking self-sovereignty.

I ask Jennifer if she would be willing to see an image of anger, to thank it for its teachings but explain that there is something else for her now. "Anger," she states, "you have a place, and I've grown through my relationship with you, but you don't rule me." Echoed in this language is the acknowledgement that even anger, typically seen in our culture as one of the darker expressions of the human condition, can help us to grow.

Her last words of the imaginal remembering experience are shared above. Soon after, she settled on the sofa and sat quietly for a few moments. Then she began to share what she'd learned from the imaginal remembering experience and how it was, if at all, different from previous ways in which she had engaged with the memory.

> The emphasis shifted. It shifted from my being stubborn and willful, the spoiled little girl going off . . . it was more of the connection. . . . It deepened, and the emotional power of it was—the love got more. . . . I was a willful little kid . . . I was hurt, too . . . I still felt the trauma of them separating . . . having my world shaken up and destroyed.

We hear in this statement the instability of her childhood foundation. Jennifer then expressed her new understanding that the walking away "wasn't a bad way to handle it. . . . I physically worked it out of my body that way, which is actually good learning because I need to remember to do that." This physical activity functions as a grounding to the earth, creating a stable connection for the first chakra; perhaps this is how "the love got more."

Jennifer also spoke about how the imaginal remembering experience allowed her to relive the "gifts" of childhood, specifically her "love of nature." We returned to this love of nature when Jennifer and I spoke about two weeks later. She expressed that, during these two weeks, she was on a retreat where she had spent time considering a dream that included "issues about abandonment." She also shared that while she was on retreat, in a moment of bodywork, the image of a wolf appeared to her. She recalled to me that in her memory, "I was the one who abandoned Dad and Patricia," and with "most of my boyfriends, I was the one who left." Abandonment is, she stated, "one of my fears, so I turned and inflicted it on other people." Jennifer saw the image of the wolf as symbolizing fear.

Pulled through the collective, through the archetypal, I also wondered if the wolf might, too, be an expression of the Greek goddess Artemis whose mother Leto shape-shifted into a she-wolf, and who herself is also associated with wolves. Artemis images an archetypal longing toward a feminine freedom, a companionship to one's self. Is it possible that both things can live alongside one another: fear of abandonment along with companionship to one's self? Just as Jennifer was called to see that escape is not always bad and anger not always wrong, perhaps too, choosing to be alone is not just about abandoning another but communing with oneself.

To Every Self, Return

We began this chapter by considering if imaginal remembering could be, in the words of James Hillman, an experience of soul-making. Soul-making, you may recall, is that psychological process in which each of us becomes more deeply aware of the self both as an individual and as part of a collective whole, one vital aspect of the greater universe. We make soul, as Edward Casey suggested, when we see into the depths of what has been. These *active remembering* excavations into the past move us forward, inviting the self to expand, by seeing through to the personal myths that have shaped and continue to shape us or by witnessing our personal journeys as permutations of greater archetypal themes. We feed the soul so that it may grow when we step outside of the limitations of a fixed past and witness ourselves as the polyvalent beings we are or as one small, albeit significant, gem in a cosmic mosaic.

The stories of Aria and Jennifer depict this kind of journeying back that takes us forward. For Aria and Jennifer, in looking backward, through the process of imaginal remembering, they witnessed the ways in which the past self, perhaps forgotten, perhaps archetypal, still lives within each of them. For each, the past self offered something: a way forward from the encouragement or forgiveness of the past. I believe this is, at least in part, due to the openness that imaginal remembering requires. By letting go, moving beyond the fixedness of what we believe once was, and allowing it to be what it is to us now, we might find a living aspect of the current and a potential for the future.

Aria's younger self, hardly a fixed remnant of the past, lives within her now as the guide who seeks to share with Aria the way through this next phase of death/rebirth. By *collecting*, as Aria words it, this younger self, she finds a confidant, a trusted adviser for the current passage along her life's journey because this younger self has been here and knows a way through. Holding hands, imagistically and metaphorically, the past and current Aria agree to work together, building a pathway for the future Aria, the self they both long to be.

With courage, Jennifer returned to a very young self, but rather than meet a spoiled and defiant child, she found a child who was grieving abandonment and doing the best she could, as a young person, to survive. This child-image, reflecting what Jennifer's mother taught her to be, is the strong and self-sufficient feminine who will get herself, alone, through life's hardships. This child still lives within Jennifer, guiding her through life's challenges. This child, who instinctually runs from those who might otherwise leave her, has also learned to run toward what is constant. In her intimate relationship with nature, Jennifer (both past and current) finds the feminine resolve depicted in the goddess Artemis, a mythical underpinning that seems to canvas the backdrop of Jennifer's life. In nature, both tender and terrible, Jennifer recognizes that her own life is but one thing in a much grander plan: her selves (the present and the past) are simultaneously significant and insignificant, just as they are meant to be.

This is the practice of imaginal remembering as soul-making: *the self actively beholding itself both in a forward and backward perspective, through imagination and remembrance.* Soul is made from what was, for what is, and to prepare for what is left to be.

CHAPTER 7

BIRTH, DEATH, AND REBIRTH: THE CYCLES OF LIFE AND SOUL

In Chapter 6 about understanding one's self through imaginal remembering, we spoke of the way in which the process makes soul through retelling the stories of our lives. The images we invite into our consciousness often appear as symbols open to amplification. Imaginal remembering enables us to gaze upon our memory-images with renewed wonder and receptivity, beholding the archetypal myths that evidence themselves in our own lives. You may recall that James Hillman called this aspect of soul-making *personifying*, where personifying beckons the ego, that which is personal and mundane, to see beyond itself, to recognize the psyche as burdened and blessed by that which is greater than the ego, that which is collective, even sacred.

> To realize that the psyche fabricates memories means to accept the reality that experiences themselves are being made by the soul out of itself and independently of the ego's engagement in its so-called real world.
> ~ James Hillman[140]

Through such in-sight, a seeing into our lives, we move towards another aspect of soul-making, what Hillman referred to as *dehumanizing*. Dehumanizing describes psyche's capacity to recognize that our soul is both within and beyond each of us. A mystifying perspective, yes, but one that offers us the freedom to see our soul's experiences as extending beyond human form. It invites us to embrace that which exists as a part of as well as exceeding our human experiences: this includes the enigmas of birth and death…what has come before and what shall come after our own existence. Creation and being, as we read in Chapter 8, necessitate extinction and non-being. So it goes, if we accept ourselves as living bodies, we must accept ourselves as dying bodies. Soul-making then, at least in part, is the soul coming to embrace its relationship to birth and death, perhaps explaining why stories of birth and death are so very soulful: the soul being so very present within them.

The memories shared in this chapter are two bookends of life: a memory of birth and a memory of death. The first is the story of Lilly who remembers and then re-members the moment her grandson was born. The memory itself is beloved, but experienced again through the phenomenon of imaginal remembering, Lilly comes even closer to the deeper meanings that live behind the event. For Julia, the breathtaking story of her father's death is further enriched by the astonishing rebirth seemingly beckoned by her imaginal remembering experience. In these stories, we find how soul seems to stretch beyond our human capacities.

The Sacred Cycle of Birth and Death: Lilly's Story

Lilly is a woman in her sixties, with thick, dark hair and a strong, regal stature. She is a therapist, an artist, and a dancer, and she moves as fluidly through these roles as she moves her body through space. I first met Lilly at a retreat. She was sitting in a white rocking chair and rose to welcome me; her large, warm hand clasped mine, and she pulled me over to a chair beside her. I immediately felt welcomed by her presence as if she knew all along I would be coming. She has that spirit about her, always curious, always open, always welcoming. She brings this same approach to dreams.

When I first spoke with her about the imaginal remembering work we had agreed to do, she confessed that her work with dream images has nurtured her faith in a higher meaning. "What happens most of the time is a kind of residual effect—a kind of resonance and connection. It hangs with you," she confided, as an experience that "softens and deepens you, that pulls you to that soft place that is comforting."

We met one cold winter morning. Just as we were settling down, large, wet flakes of snow began to fall from the grey skies, landing on the branches of Ponderosa Pines that stood taller than the second story apartment where Lilly and I worked that morning. We both commented on the falling snow before quieting ourselves for the brief meditation that had become a customary part of these sessions. When the soft bell sounded the close of this first meditation, Lilly turned toward me and announced that she wished to make "a brief little statement about where we're going." It was if Lilly once again reached out and grabbed my hand.

Her grandmother, Lilly explained, would "be present in some way." I knew that Lilly had never *met* her grandmother, a woman from Eastern Europe who had lived through the hardships of having her world torn apart by both World Wars. I also knew this hadn't kept Lilly from sharing a deep and meaningful connection with her grandmother's spirit. As it turns out, her first conscious connection with that spirit had occurred a few years prior, at a moment in the day when the snow had first begun to fall.

The memory she described was of "a very powerful experience...etched in my memory. . . . Sacred." It recalled the original event of Lilly's youngest grandchild's birth some four or more years before we met this day. Lilly believed that the sacredness of the memory called her to it for it was an experience that "touched my life." She shared:

> When I entered the room, it was in my daughter and son-in-law's home, upstairs in their bedroom. They had a midwife there. I got there, just as [the baby's] head was crowning. And I opened the door, and the room was full of a golden glow from the candle. . . . That's what I remember the most, is the glow of the candle. It just opened up the room, and [it] was so full of warmth, and a welcoming, and

a sacred place. . . . I observed this beautiful human being coming into this world. I think I was surprised at how he looked because sometimes you have a sense of what the baby might be looking like. He had really large eyes, and I wasn't aware of anyone having these really large bright eyes, beautiful eyes. . . . After he was born, I welcomed [my eldest grandchild] into the room. He held the baby . . . he was quite present and in awe even though he didn't say it. . . . After he came into the room then I went to get [my granddaughter] . . . I believe she was already awake, and I went to welcome her. . . . When you have a midwife, when they weigh the baby, it's in a cloth. The hands don't have any plastic on them, no gloves or anything. So what touched him first was life, and skin on skin. And then they lifted up the weighing cloth, I guess you would say just to see how much he weighed. And they did the measurements, and I guess they made sure everything is fine which of course he was.

There was little to clarify about Lilly's memory. My primary questions were of names of those present, ages of the children, and when the memory had taken place.

I explained to Lilly that we would meditate again, and after that I would ask her to share the memory as a living image. To this, Lilly responded, "Okay. I'm not totally clear on what that means, how it's different from the first time." I shared with her my belief that the image would come forward as she shared it with me. Like a dream, the memory would open so long as we were present to the memory-images. I invited her to let the images lead her to whatever they wished to share, whatever wisdom they sought to impart. We both seemed to have a trust in Lilly's openness to the memory-images and their reciprocated openness towards her.

Lilly enters into the imaginal remembering experience by placing herself at the stairs of her daughter's home, "walking up the stairs, and opening the door." Her return to the memory is swift, where she describes it, start to finish, in less than two minutes. I recognize that there is a hunger to move quickly to the climax of the memory, the birth of Lionel, her grandson. I also recognize the most exquisite things often need time and space to fully reveal themselves.

I ask Lilly to come back into the memory, but, this time, I encourage her to slow down, taking the time to feel into her body. She notes that her body is "full of wonderment." She exudes excitement and anxiety, rushing toward the door, toward the sacred phenomenon of the birth. I acknowledge to her that this space holds profound meaning; it is an invitation into the presence of life itself. But because I sense that the memory-image is calling to be approached gently, deliberately, I suggest to Lilly that she return to the memory-image, inviting her to walk slowly back up the stairs. I ask her to witness what's there; to look around it as an animate and autonomous image, as the living image that I believe it is.

With this suggestion, Lilly becomes very aware of the psychic environment of the memory-image; "it's dark" and she is "moving through the darkness, step by step," in wonderment of what follows the darkness. With prompting, Lilly waits on the landing feeling her feet standing and her hand at the doorknob. Though she is prepared to turn the knob, she just holds it, feeling "a sense of excitement" in her hand. The knob, she describes,

> The hands . . .[evoke] a kind of shamanic permeability of human, animal and spirit worlds.
> ~ Ami Ronnberg[141]

"feels soft, and it feels light" (even though it was metal) as if there's a "buffer between my hand and the door knob."

She now feels "warmth . . . lightness, but my feet are on the ground. I feel my feet, my heart, and my hand on the doorknob." Staying here, on the other side of this "miracle," Lilly notices that "there's a mystery . . . the curiosity veil of what's behind it and a desire to open the door and find out." Soon she opens the door and is stunned by the image. "It's a sight to behold," a word chosen as if to express this very precious moment that Lilly carries within her psyche—what *is* will be *held*.

"The walls are glistening. There is a kind of beating . . . a heartbeat. . . . It's amazing to me that this little candle can put out so much light." The birthplace room appears alive, beating, in the glistening illumination of the small candle's light. The light is illuminating "this crowning of the infant . . . guiding the movement of the crowning of his head as he moves out, as he moves up." I note to myself that in the Berber culture of North Africa, a lamp was placed near a baby's head when born, the flame of the lamp signifying the spirit of the divine glowing within this new being.[142]

Lilly hears the baby's cry, "a feminine sound," and sees his "big bright eyes, and a small little body. It's just incredible." She acknowledges the "privilege of being there and experiencing the miracle." I watch as her hand reaches out into the air. In the memory-image, her hand moves towards him to "caress . . . [the] magic of [him, specifically his head], it's solid, and yet it's so beautiful." She notices that the same "soft cushion" experienced between her hand and the doorknob is now felt between her hand and Lionel's head.

She sees a "glow around him, kind of like a Christ-like glow that you see in churches, just an aura." What Lilly seems to describe here is an aureole that may symbolize a spiritual light that emanates from a physical being.[143] This glow is "full of energy" and seems to grow as a "plain energy"; it's "lightening my body" and "[I] feel it around me." She questions whether this is her grandmother, that her grandmother's spirit was also present during the birth of Lionel.

Tears fall from Lilly's eyes as she whispers, "It's touching to feel her…and to know that she will always be there, and that she's always there." "In awe," Lilly recognizes that "in this moment [of imaginal remembering], being present, but at that moment [of the original event] not having been as deep." She questions if "maybe slowing down the experience" deepens the experience. She also may have been every bit as deep in the original event, just not at a conscious level: the body being an extraordinary reservoir of our past experiences, it often absorbs what the conscious mind does not.

Soon after this realization, Lilly describes a "cloud-like image" of her grandmother where the presence of her spirit connects, for Lilly, "the cycle of life and death. Birth. Death. Birth." Clouds, unbeknownst to Lilly, may symbolize a manifestation of the divine—a cloud is an exchange between earth and air, a comingling of what is earthly and what is ethereal.[144]

The grandmother-like cloud shifts to more clouds that then shift into a large winged bird that Lilly believes is there to "offer protection, to be a guardian" and to offer "guidance." Indeed, the bird symbolizes the soul and the breath of the world, but Lilly shares more which further deepens the amplification. "It isn't the shape of an eagle, but it feels like an eagle flying over, and just kind of protecting from the elements, creating safety, a safe space, keeping faith, being warm, being present to life, feeling honored." Unconscious to Lilly, the eagle is a symbol of the hero, the father, the patriarchy.[145] Lilly is then drawn to an image of a breast (which represents motherhood as well as feminine wisdom, nourishment, and survival in the earthly realm[146]).

The breast-image coupled with the eagle-image appear to represent a *coniunctio*, a sacred union, of mother, feminine, earth, soul with father, masculine, sky, spirit. These archetypal images living in Lilly's memory are pregnant with meaning and sacredness even though Lilly is unconscious of their explicit significance.

What Lilly does note are Lionel's "big beautiful eyes," which are "both innocent and wise." They draw her attention toward "another eye . . . a large eye opening up, looking upward. Bright, a lot of light . . . sunshine." She feels the sunshine-image in her hands and through her body, bringing "light and warmth" and "breaking through the clouds . . . warm[ing] the earth." With this, Lilly, on her own, moves out of the memory-image, noting that "I feel like I'm coming back into the earth." The dissipation of the cloud and the sunshine that move through her body as energy seem to allow her passage from what she has experienced as the spiritual, divine realm back into the physical world.

Soon Lilly opened her eyes and rubbed her hands along the tops of her thighs as if reconnecting to her physical body. She looked at me, smiling in her welcoming way, and then we began to discuss her imaginal remembering experience. She described that to be present to the memory in this way was "deeper; it's like surreal; I wasn't aware of that memory in the same way." For her to experience the memory as she did, imaginally, she acknowledged that she had to leave what was "'concrete;' this is not concrete." The memory of the event was "the way it was experienced in my physical body; I left my physical body." For example, she had not held her grandson, Lionel, in the original event, but during the imaginal remembering, she was quite

aware of cradling the newborn. By moving out of the memory as
"concrete," it "deepens my experience with myself and the sacred."

Let's pause and consider the idea that Lilly is referencing the
physical body differently than I have been. I would argue she is not
referring specifically to her body as it is now but as she remembers it
moving in the original event, the way in which it physically engaged
with the material world around it to include Lionel. Indeed, as she
remembers the event, her physical body did not cradle him as she
cradled the baby-image in the imaginal remembering session. Yet, we
must acknowledge that Lilly's physical body was an ally in deepening
her experience; she didn't leave the physical body, rather she left the
physical realm's dictates of how her physical body behaved.

Here's the crux: it's necessary, in imaginal remembering, to
loosen the binds of the physical world in terms of what we believe
physically happened. But, because the living images are embodied (as
you recall from Chapter 1), we cannot dismiss our physical being as
we engage in imaginal remembering—profound presence to our
soma is a primary way in which we experience the living images of
our psyche.

Lilly's engagement with her soma, her body, helped her drop into
the imaginal experience. Our physical bodies, when given the chance,
allow us to meet and experience the non-physical world, be that the
spirit or imaginal realm. They absorb and store a great deal of the
energy that moves through us at a psychological level even if we do
not feel their movement as related to the physical world.

For Lilly, moving into a nonphysical realm, out of the physical
body, and becoming present to "boundless energy," the experience is
one of "life and death. It's an experience; it's still really a mystery,
both being born and dying." For Lilly, it is "a miracle that our minds
don't really get, but the energy is the same. It's an exchange. But it's
not a physical energy, it's a different energy." This energy is like what
Eastern philosophies describe as the *subtle body*, which is separate
from the physical body. Our mind (separate from our brain) and our
ego are present in the subtle body, and for this reason, the subtle
body may be reborn into another physical body. The subject of Lilly's
memory, the original event that forms it, regards the birth of Lionel.
In the imaginal remembering experience, her grandmother's spirit,
someone no longer of this world, is also present. Birth and death
coexist.

Lilly also sensed the session would impact her in the physical world, offering her "tolerance and understanding, compassion and moving slower." She related the idea of "moving slower" to tolerance and compassion because "I think we are quick to judge. . . . It's a reminder to me there are grey areas." This idea of moving slower became even more pronounced in the weeks between the imaginal remembering session and our final interview. She "had more of an appreciation of needing to be present in life . . . slowing down."

This slowing down has offered her more attentiveness to her grandchildren, the environments around her, even the beauty of the colors of the world. "Just [to] be more deliberate and really, that slowing down is important. It really is because the memories they stay with you, and they are imprinted." In this act of being more present to what's happening, she described being non-judgmental about the present and the future themselves, opening herself up to what is not yet known. This has helped her specifically with the difficult idea that soon her daughter and grandchildren may be geographically relocating many hours away from Lilly. Practicing slowing down has allowed her to "just to stay present, to what is now, and who knows what will happen."

Lilly also recalled that during the imaginal remembering experience, her hands were a vehicle for deepening into the experience. "There's creativity in my hands . . . and it is about creativity. Lionel was created by God you know on a larger level." It appears that Lilly has tied the creativity of her hands to the fundamental idea of the cycle of life. For her, creativity is what "makes me feel alive, but I didn't realize how important my hands were." In returning to the idea of moving slower, Lilly described "being aware of creativity taking its time, and needing to take its time." A desire, as I noted, of the memory-image itself.

In closing, Lilly returned to a symbol that appeared during the imaginal remembering session. She explained the value of being present to the living images.

Having more faith in the energy of life that it ebbs and flows, kind of like a bird. It's important, for me, to understand that you can glide and take advantage of what life offers, and then every once in a while, you hit some bumps. But it doesn't mean you can't glide anymore. Glide in a different direction I guess. Sometimes a lot better. For me, that's the way [imaginal remembering] is, is that it opens up awareness and creates new experiences internally.

The bird, as we saw earlier, is a symbol of the soul. We might then intuit that Lilly is describing the wanderings and deepening of the soul throughout life and its experiences, especially when we take the time for reflection.

Endings and Beginnings: Julia Story's

Julia is one the most cheerful people I've ever met. With short dark hair and a warm smile, it's easy to spend time in her company. But that easiness is not something that simply arrives for Julia. She is earnest about making connections with others, ensuring she knows about your life because she cares about your life. She feels simultaneously like a dear friend and a surrogate mother: laughing and crying with you. She has made a life around caring for children, and when you get to know her, you can understand why. She seems to have an innate ability to encourage even the smallest parts of ourselves. Perhaps that is because she is careful to be aware of and pay attention to everything.

Julia and I met for our imaginal remembering session one sunny morning. She welcomed me into her office which is situated on the second floor of historic building in the downtown district of an old mining town. It has a pillowy sofa and a plush, comfortably worn chair. Paintings from local artists trim the walls. I immediately felt at ease taking a seat on the sofa, she in the chair. After a brief chat about our lives, she confessed that she had not yet chosen a memory. Like others, she asked for clarification of how she should select one, and I explained that the only criteria were that it was of a personal lived-event and that it seemed to say, "Come spend some time with me." I suggested we share a brief mediation in which something might come to her. When the moment of silence had ended, I asked her what memory brought us together, and she replied.

I had several, but the one that really crystallized for me was actually my father's passing. . . . It was 2008 or 2009, but it's very vivid still. When I closed my eyes, as sometimes I'm lucky enough to do, I'll see an eye, and this very much seemed like my dad saying, "Yeah." . . . I don't speak to him as much as I'd like to. So, he must just want to come in today.

Given that the eye is often associated as the window of soul, perhaps Julia was connecting with what she perceived as her father's spirit or soul, given that he is no longer of this world. She then proceeded to recall the memory.

I was spending the night in Southern California in the bedroom that I grew up in my parents' home, and my mother came to the door and said, "Your dad says get up." So, I got up, and he was lying down in the living room, where he had been for a long time, and he said, "Get out a pen and paper." I said, "Okay." He said, "I want you to write this down."

As she recalled, Julia wrote down the obituary her father dictated and then called her brothers (who lived nearby), also as her father directed, because he believed this would be the day he would die. She continued:

Within an hour or two, they all gathered, and some of my nieces and nephews all were there. And my dad was laying on the couch, [with] all these people around, and he said, "Well, so what are we waiting for?" "I don't know, Dad. What do you think?" And he said, "Well, could you move that table away?" He was speaking so symbolically at this point. No medication. "Could you move that table away because I want to make the way clear?"

The three brothers removed the table, took him to the bathroom, and then waited. Julia recalled how she found their work together particularly meaningful given that Julia and her two younger brothers are estranged from their older brother, Rusty. As time went by, family members started scattering across the residence both inside and outside. Julia then noted:

> All of a sudden I hear this outbreath. It was like that really high shrill . . . and my image was of an arrow shooting up into space. And it was his last breath, and he died with everybody around. And it was amazing.

Family members began to pay their respects. Julia recalled saying, "'Oh my god, Dad, thank you for showing me how to die. I can do it, if this is what it is. . . . It doesn't have to be scary, and you've got all your family around.'" While Julia rejoiced in the profoundness of the experience, watching her dad pass into what she described as "beyond the veil," she also recalled, "there was a lot of flak after that with people thinking I'm the wacky sister."

When she finished sharing the memory, Julia and I spoke about the details. She explained that her father's health had been deteriorating due to heart failure despite a pacemaker that had been implanted recently. Not long before his death, he had been discharged from the hospital because there was nothing else medically to be done and his desire was to be home.

Julia had prepared herself for his passing, reading a book that explained a person whose life is waning often speaks symbolically. Julia found this to be true for her dad: in one example, he explained, "The electricity's going to go out in the house, and I don't think I'm going to be able to put it back on again," despite no electrical issues in the home. For Julia, this experience of watching her dad as he drifted "in and out of behind that veil" was mysterious and fascinating, possibly because of her belief in past lives.

She encouraged her father to do what he needed to do when he explained to her, "'You know Julia, you came down here to help me to get better, and I'm just not getting better.' I said, 'Dad I came to just be with you, and whatever is, I came to just be with you.'" She remembered asking her dad, "'Are you afraid?'" He explained that he wasn't but was also unsure if there was anything else. He wished he "'believe[d] like you believe'" in some great beyond, but such philosophy was counter to his scientific mind. Although he did not judge Julia for her beliefs, she noted that she felt her family saw her as "'crazy, woohoo, nutty Julia,' totally."

This theme of taking "flak" and being judged seemed to have weight, and so I asked Julia if that was something that needed to be expressed during our session. "Maybe a bit," she said, "because it still hurts." Even though the memory regards the compelling moment of her father's death, it also appears, even at the outset, to be about much more. Julia herself called the memory "profound" and "poignant." *Profound* is derived from the Latin terms *pro* meaning before and *fundus* meaning deep, bottomless, and vast. *Poignant* is from the Latin word *pungere* meaning to prick or pierce. In this way, we might see that Julia herself recognized that entering the memory imaginally might break open into a boundless space yet unrealized. As we closed our conversation to meditate before tending the memory, Julia noted that perhaps this memory had come to her this day because it will soon be her father's birthday or "maybe it's [about] healing with my older brother [Rusty]. I have no clue."

Julia, like other participants, first enters the memory-image by telling the memory to me much in the same way she earlier recalled it. When she is finished, we begin again with my prompting to be present to the images and her own body in a way that embodies the experience even by physically moving. Julia takes this suggestion and begins to move around her office as though she is in the image of her childhood home. She describes her bedroom as lilac, the same color it was when she was a child, though she believes it is now another color. "But," she says, "somehow that lilac's important." It is as if Julia knows that lilac, a hue of purple, is the last color of the rainbow and is thereby associated with dying by connecting what is known to what is unknown.[147]

She moves through the memory-image, at first making eye contact with her mother-image, who fetches her on behalf of her dad. In her mother, Julia sees "her age and her worry, but also her strength." While the mother and daughter share a moment of gratitude, the energy of the memory-image does not exist between the two because Julia feels the urge to go to her father-image.

She takes down the dictation of his obituary, and as she does this a second time, she does it with full presence to the memory-image, noting that the image of her father is sitting up "very businesslike." In spending time here, she admits he is both "warm and strong, and also feeble and gray" holding these opposites and hearing him explain to her that "it's been a good life." Both Julia and her dad acknowledge it is his time to go. "He's just resolved," she notes. The term *resolve* derives from the Latin word *resolvere,* meaning to unyoke or unbind, in this case, presumably from the physical world. But for Julia, it also means he is strong enough to deal with death, able to endure the pain of the body. She recalls that as a child he would take from her and her siblings their illnesses so that they would heal, or so she, as a little girl, believed.

She notices, as she is speaking with him, that he's squinting the way he does when he is "looking far out to find an answer." What he shares with Julia is that "it is pretty amazing" to be in a place that is other than the physical world. She asks him what it's like to be where he is, and why he sometimes seems to come back to her, and her mother and brothers. She worries that he is "clinging to . . . this world" but also acknowledges that his visits are quite meaningful to her. As she speaks with him, he responds that "'you were more right than you think . . . you're onto something.'" For Julia, this "feels very powerful" as his comment validates her beliefs.

His acknowledgement of Julia appears to be an opening because, at this point, the conversation moves to the image of her father sharing that "all this stuff that we get caught up in is so silly, when it's just about love." This stuff, Julia acknowledges, is "war . . . and . . . strife" but it is also "even me and my brother. 'It's just nonsense'" she hears her father say, "'at the end of the day it's just heart to heart, person to person.'" Of this she shares, "I'm really kind of getting this message that maybe it's time for me to try and let go" of the challenges she has with her brother Rusty. "Regardless of how I need him when I need him and he's drinking . . . just to try to be soul to soul, sister to brother." Before we entered the memory-image, Julia shared with me that her father was and Rusty is an alcoholic. As an adult, Julia learned to accept and forgive her father's alcoholism, but she finds her brother to be "too toxic." Further, when she first told me the memory of her father's death, she ended it by describing, "He knew how to let go. He knew how to let go." Perhaps then Julia's dad-image is here to help her, as she says, "try to let go" of the pain associated with Rusty.

Julia asks for her dad-image's advice in trying to mend the relationship with Rusty and Julia hears that it is not something that can really be contrived. Rather, he tells her to "just meet each encounter in that moment, just right then . . . just give it a chance." She then tells herself to "take it as it comes, and realize he's got his demons . . . maybe not to judge him so much. Just to be curious, or if nothing else, compassionate and open-minded."

She recalls that her dad, quite to the amazement of his doctor, "grew a pathway," another artery when one of his arteries to the heart had become clogged. He explained to the doctor, and to Julia, that "'I just needed to be able to visualize it.'" This idea of a pathway appears originally in the telling of the memory, when her father asks for the table to be moved to clear a path. When I ask Julia to consider if the "heart to heart" she has been experiencing with her dad might offer her a pathway towards healing with Rusty, she shares, "I immediately see my brother Rusty, and I go and hug him. He's got tears, I've got tears, and he just said, 'I'm sorry.'" Julia too apologizes, and she notes that, in the physical world, they rarely hugged.

She is torn with the present image because she feels that she has forgiven Rusty before only to be disappointed. When she consults her dad-image, he explains, "'I'm doing everything that I can, and all of you have to do this work. . . . It's yours to do.'" Julia acknowledges this has been something "I've been trying to avoid."

She returns to the image of her dad, visualizing the artery, and says, "I'm getting the sense that meditating and centering and sending some attention for healing might be really powerful." At this point she notices a "golden cord or something" that connects her to her father-image. Skeptical that she is just making this up in her head, she attempts to sever the cord but finds that it cannot be cut. Recognizing that perhaps on an imaginal level she can make a difference, she sees this cord connecting to her other brothers as well.

With prompting, she looks into each of the images of her brothers' eyes, beginning with Rusty. As she does this, she notices "a wound" from "when he was 20"; Rusty and his fiancé, Lydia, were in a car accident in which Lydia died. Julia notes, "It's really him standing here because I hadn't thought about that."

She recalls remembering the night of Lydia's death. Julia was asleep but awoke to see Lydia enter through the front door and kiss Rusty on the cheek, "and then she, like, evaporated." Julia remembered a tear rolled from Rusty's bandaged eye. Several minutes later, her father came home to share the news that Lydia had passed.

As Julia tells me of this memory, she then notes that the image of Rusty "is so thankful," sharing that Julia "is onto something" regarding an afterlife. He tells his sister, "I was judgmental and wrong." Julia comes to understand that this tragic experience is likely what started Rusty down the path of alcoholism. Still, she is afraid that he will hurt her again, but he asks her to "try, I might surprise you. I will surprise you." With this she asks him to see her as she is and not what he has projected on her. She realizes that she too must stop her projecting.

Julia now notices that the image of Rusty is stepping back, her father's image having been "observing in a serious, wise, solid way" her engagement with Rusty. She makes a connection with her other brothers, though it would appear there is less energy with them in this memory-image. We close the experience with several minutes of observed quiet.

When the meditation had ended, Julia explained that, in those moments of quiet, she spoke again with her father, and saw her mother and younger brothers fade. She imagined a meeting with Rusty, sharing, "Now when I do see Rusty, I want to know it will all be heart to heart, and I'll be visualizing that." For her, this aspect of reconnecting with her brother has "added to" the original event, what was already a very "sacred, wonderful experience that was perfect all by itself." In this way, the imaginal remembering experience "takes it forward."

Julia admitted that she'd "written off" her relationship with Rusty, but entering the memory as an image has "opened the door to considering" whether this is the best approach. As she noted, she still holds resentment towards her brother, and "you know, they say holding resentment is like you drinking poison and hoping they die." In this way, it is as if she is acknowledging that experiencing a "cut-off" relationship with Rusty has been toxic for her. "It's a birth family," she shared. "We're all there for a reason, so it's like I'd be giving up on learning the lesson or deepening the lesson, and maybe that is really important, even more important than I think or had thought before."

When Julia and I met again by phone a few weeks later, she told me that over these weeks, she's dedicated time to meditation and imaging that connection with her brother. Following the imaginal remembering session, she explained, "I just had a softening so that I realized his pain and the dysfunction that he's in. I just had more compassion for it." The word *compassion* is derived from the past participle Latin word *compati*, where *com* means together and *pati* means to suffer. Julia here expresses her willingness to suffer with her brother rather than to stand apart from his suffering.

She built upon her description of "softening," stating that she "had a melting there" toward him. Julia's language intimates an alchemical process of the psyche, something that C.G. Jung extensively studied in his later years.[148,149] Jung's works, which have been deepened by others, express the exquisite metaphor of alchemy that keenly symbolizes the psychological death/rebirth process. Here, Julia's language of "softening" and "melting" seem to alchemically describe a shift of the ego, perhaps a rebirth of the ego.

Soon after sharing this with me, Julia described a dream she had the night before where she's in her childhood home (the home where the original event of her father's passing took place). In the dream, her father is "remodeling the kitchen" right at the "threshold from the living room where he died, which borders on the kitchen." In Julia's imaginal remembering experience, she hugged the image of Rusty, her "estranged" brother, in this location. Further, in the dream, "there is painting and stuff on the patio . . . and some clients that were trying to reach me and couldn't quite get me." She later explained feeling in her dream "a little apologetic for not being prompt" for her clients, who were standing in the living room. She also remembers feeling "a little unsettled, like 'What am I doing?'"

Julia admitted that if it were not for our call this day, she might not have considered the meaning of the dream. We spoke about what the dream might have been telling Julia. Notably, her father is "remodeling" the kitchen, reshaping that part of the home that, as you might recall from Chapter 6, may symbolize the transformation of the self. Furthermore, the location of the remodeling, the space in which she reconnected with her brother, the threshold between the kitchen and the living room where her father died, seems to image that alchemical rebirth that perhaps was foretold in Julia's language of her own "softening," her own "melting" toward her brother. There, too, is reconstruction of the patio, a threshold from the inner and outer of the home. This may hint at Julia's reformation with her brother, a process that is first beginning in her inner, imaginal world, before it moves to the outer, physical world.

It is difficult to say what the dream means regarding her clients waiting in the living room, but that Julia is late, "unsettled," and questioning of herself, suggests that her new space of being open to a reconnection with her brother has her slightly off kilter and feeling unprepared. These emotions certainly are understandable. It may even suggest a need for her to show compassion to herself (along with the compassion she intends to have for Rusty) for the mistakes she feels she has already made including being "late" to forgive Rusty. Or it may also symbolize the uncertainty she may feel along this journey of a rebirthed relationship.

We closed our conversation by discussing the way in which the experience may impact the relationships she has with others, including her father and herself. She noted missing both her brother and father, enjoying their interest in the sciences. She mentioned that the discovery of gravitational waves in the universe (a discovery that occurred between the imaginal remembering session and this final interview) was a topic she would have liked to have discussed with them.

A colleague of hers at work, a man she described as "very heady and scientific," explained to her that such a discovery suggested, at least for him, "'that no memories are lost. . . . And the whole concept of reincarnation and all that's been lived and dreamed and thought about everything still exists." She considered his interpretation relative to what we had been discussing and contemplated the possibility that the work we had done and that she has continued to do is also "sending out ripples." Recalling and then imaginally engaging with this "big memory" becomes the opportunity to "make some changes and cause a shift in a real relationship" even though that work is at an imaginal level. "I'm just really thankful for the opportunity because I think it helps me grow, too."

From my perspective, the gravitational waves discovery in juxtaposition to Julia's experience is quite intriguing: in the imaginal remembering experience, she reached back into the past, connected with a man who is no longer of this physical world, and made and continues to make a connection with an estranged brother, a connection that may impact her future. The experience seems to both be within and creating a ripple.

When the Soul Stands at the Edge

In working with our psychic images through the process of imaginal remembering, we plumb the depths of the soul, all the while soul-making, by looking backward and forward—fully active, fully imaginative, and fully open to what each direction shares with us about ourselves and our souls. To invite these vantage points to extend beyond our human experience . . . to gaze upon the beginnings and endings of life, witnessing the moments of birth and death, catching glimpses of what seems to precede and exceed our awareness . . . here, too, we find soul.

> Soul-making, we can conclude, is ineluctably a remembering, while remembering is itself a main means of reversion to the soul.
> ~ Edward Casey[150]

In her imaginal remembering experience of Lionel's birth, Lilly is called to witness the sacredness of her own life as it exists every day. Lilly's story teaches us that when we approach life with slow, attentive movements, we may find that each day holds the possibilities of creation and extinction, arrivals and departures.

Julia's story begins as the remembrance of losing her father, yet it ends as a re-collecting of her estranged brother. Her imaginal remembering experience invites Julia into a resurrected relationship with Rusty, even if that relationship exists within her own psyche. As Julia herself explained to me, the meaningfulness of connecting with her father's memory-image exists, in part, because she's connected to the wisest part of her own self where this self is revealed in the living images of her ancestors. As her story seems to suggest, the wisdom that extends beyond our human existence also lives within us.

We have come to know imaginal remembering as a practice that seems to move us into a deeper relationship with our soul because it invites us to witness each of our lives as something greater than our individual stories. It takes courage to enter the imaginal, accepting what is not physically real as also having value. We're often frightened by the unknown, and the living images of our own psyche can be of deepest mystery. It is then quite intriguing to me that imaginal remembering may also invite us to wander to the margins, the beginnings and endings of our physical existence. Here, we lean just a bit, taking a peak over the edges and pausing to consider what might exist before and after our own human existence. It seems to offer us the uncanny gift of witnessing the mysteries that stand beyond each and all our lives.

CHAPTER 8

FORGIVING AND LETTING GO: THE MEMORIES OF THOSE WE'VE LOST

The existentialist psychologist Rollo May wrote often on the subject to death. He argued that it was the binary other to *being*: death as the *no-being* that cannot be escaped.[151] As human *beings*, we are intimately aware that our bodies are only on loan to us. What we can count on is that, at some point, we will cease to exist, at least as we do now. While this produces anxiety in some (directly or indirectly), others are bolstered by the thought. May writes of one patient who, fearing an upcoming presentation in which he thought he might be judged harshly, rationalized to himself that, someday, we shall all be dead, so what was the point of sweating the small stuff?

Maybe it's easier for us to accept death when it feels far from us. Conceptual thinking is different than emotional experiencing, so it stands to reason, we might better accept the concept of our own death than we accept the reality of our beloveds dying. We often endure tremendous grief and sadness for the loved one, especially when their end of life is filled with pain and suffering or their death is abrupt or absurd. Perhaps, too, we grieve the loss of part of our self, the one who existed in relationship to the one whom we are losing or have already lost. The life of this self, entwined with the life of the deceased, no longer exists. The psychiatrist Roland Kuhn explained that when we mourn the loss of a beloved, we often experience that grief as the inability to *depart the departed*.[152] We become stuck in their absence. He described it as a *being-together* with the deceased which necessitates that we, as mourners, *be* with the deceased in the only way we can: through our intrapsychic images of them, particularly as memories. He suggested that the remedy to such stuck-ness is for the self who remains to move on. But to where and how, especially if unfinished business persists?

I believe one way is to meet, in the deeper recesses of the psyche, images of the other who has passed or is passing on and our self who seems to be stuck there with them. When we approach our memories imaginally, rather than just watching the films on a big screen as the Counting Crows' lyric suggests, we

> If dreams are like movies,
> memories are films about ghosts.
> ~ Counting Crows

enter them like an actor on the stage. In this way, we invite these ghosts onto the stage with us, and these figures of our past become alive. Some may believe we are, indeed, engaging with spirits of our loved ones who now exist beyond the veil. Others may vehemently protest such an idea. I would argue that spirit or not, these stories suggest that when we return, through imaginal remembering, to the images of those we have lost, something profound occurs for the self who remains and must journey on without them.

The first story, Anne's story, based on a memory more than fifty years ago, helps us to understand that love and forgiveness still matter even if, especially if, we no longer share this world together. In the second story, Francis engaged with two memories which appear closely linked, each seeming to point her toward letting go, both of her mother who is leaving this world and to her father whose unexpected passing left unfinished business.

Forgiving Others and Ourselves: Anne's Story

I fondly recall a time when Anne and I sat together on the trunk of a fallen tree, talking about the idea of community, and how I needed to find that in the town I'd recently come to call home. A woman in her early sixties with long blond hair, Anne has taught me the value of community and the importance of relationship through both her words and her actions. I have witnessed the depths of Anne's resolve to stay in community with her family despite circumstances that would otherwise keep them apart. I have known her to be affronted by some of the most unimaginably difficult situations, and yet never give in to what tries to break the ties that bind.

She told me once that she values working with what she calls the "scary images" of her dreams because she believes these images "are the helpers" where "there is an inner part of me that is trying to resolve an issue . . . they speak the loudest to me; I listen to them the most rather than the quieter parts." This willingness to tend to what is difficult and to know it will bring resolution presented itself that late afternoon in which we engaged together in imaginal remembering.

The sun was already setting in the grey winter sky as I drove the winding road to Anne's house where she'd offered to participate in the imaginal remembering session with me. It is situated in a forest on the side of a mountain, peaceful and reserved, not unlike the woman herself. We sat in front of a wood-burning fireplace, me on the sofa, Anne in her rocker, and Bailey, her dog, at her feet.

She shared with me that the memory which seemed to call her attention was of a long-ago life experience that she hadn't "resolved." She believed the original event occurred when she was a young child, perhaps five to seven years of age. The memory "popped out," and she felt there was "no choice" as to whether it would be imaginally engaged. It seemed to call to her because it was "painful" and sought resolution. She referred to it as "undone . . . not finished for me" where other things in her life are "coming to closure." She acknowledged that she'd "always tried to figure out that relationship" between her father and brother, describing the relationship as having both a "dark . . . sad, scary part" as well as a "fun part."

Though her brother was about twelve when this remembered event took place, the relationship between father and son, as Anne recalled, worsened as her brother got older; there was a "conflict" that Anne "never understood . . . never got answers." As we continued to speak about it, and I listened to Anne's words, tone, and body language, I too felt that memory-image was seeking resolution which likely contributed to my own questions and direction during the imaginal remembering phase of our conversation.

I have found over my work that the time spent sharing the memory is much briefer than the time to engage with it as an image. This is especially true for Anne, whose memory was briefly communicated as follows:

> There's a memory of my dad and my brother, and they're in the stairway at our farm house that I grew up in. . . . We just got home from [a] meeting or gathering, and we were going to bed and it was late and we were going upstairs, and the door was open to the stairway. My dad and my brother were in the stairway, and they were laughing, and I think our folks just wanted us to go to bed. Then, [Dad] was urging [my brother] to go upstairs with his feet and goofing around, to begin with. Then, it seemed to shift into this place of my brother . . . crying, and then my dad wouldn't stop, and my mom was standing with me and my sisters, my two sisters . . . I was standing at the bottom looking up and getting scared that I didn't know what was going on because they were laughing just a bit ago, and then [my brother] was crying. . . . It wasn't a traumatic memory, and I've always had the memory. I didn't have a hard time remembering it or anything. But, there are incidents like that with my dad and my brother that seemed to just happen, and it was always like this confusion of "What's that all about? Why does that happen?" I think, if anything, in my childhood that was like the unanswered events surrounding them.

In clarifying the memory, Anne wasn't sure which of her four sisters were present during the event, but she clearly recalled the presence of her father, brother, and mother. Although her mother is still living, Anne's brother, Harry, and her father have since passed. The way in which she spoke of them, and what she said, made it appear that she was very close to both men. Before Harry passed, Anne asked him about his relationship with their father and learned that they were "okay." Still, Anne felt that Harry hadn't been treated well, that "in my heart connection with him, he's always left out. . . . It seemed to me, from watching him, all of his life was like a tortured life in so many ways."

Anne appears to blame herself for Harry being left out or at least not addressing what she felt was a wrong. "I feel like I didn't listen. I didn't open up because I was afraid or scared of what might have been said." This sense of blame lingers even after Harry's passing, as Anne admitted:

> Even now after his death and after being gone a while, it still bothers me that I never asked him what it was like. . . . When I saw [the remembered event], when I was there watching, I never asked him, "Why did he do that? Why did Dad do that to you?" It makes me cringe when I think of what it used to be.

As she spoke of this, I asked her where and how she felt this emotion in her body. "Tight inside; it's like it squeezes. . . . It's my heart." The heart chakra is the subtle body center of both grief and compassion; it is where we somatically encounter love, relationship, and balance in our lives. It is not surprising then that Anne, who throughout our conversation spoke of a deep and abiding connection and love for her brother Harry, felt the troublesome quality of the memory in the location of the heart chakra, specifically as something that was squeezing, as if the twisted points of energy of this chakra were quite knotted.

As with all participants, I asked Anne to return to the memory, but this time seeing it as a memory-image. In this way, it would invite and allow the memory to shift and reshape based on its autonomous and wise capacity.

Anne immediately begins to see the image of her sister Jane and her mother with her at the base of the staircase witnessing what begins as a playful event. When the emotions shift to something darker, Anne yells at her father for him to stop. With my nudging, she yells again this time more forcefully but admits that he "doesn't listen. . . . I don't think Dad even hears me saying that."

Anne notes, "I am standing there just in amazement. I am standing next to Mom. I think I reached out to touch her." Though touching her mom helps, it's not enough comfort for Anne. Soon Anne retreats from the memory-image as is hinted at by her language "reached out"; its past-tense intimates the movement from experiencing the image as a present phenomenon to recalling it as a past event.

I ask Anne to return into the memory as an image, but this time with the encouragement to notice what catches her eyes; to be *in* it, noticing everything around her. She indicates that it's only Harry and her father who catch her attention because "I'm trying to make sense of it." Hearing this as a deeper entrance into the memory-image, I ask Anne who in the memory-image can make sense of it for her. At this point, there is a movement for Anne from passivity as the observer to assertiveness as someone who will directly seek out answers, a resolution.

She's first inclined to seek information from the image of her mother. She starts again into the memory-image, witnessing it again from the beginning. I encourage her to see herself as the little girl and to be fully embodied as that self. Agreeing, she laughs along at first with the playful aspect of the beginning of the event, noting that her body "feels freer." However, she notices a tenseness in her mother that puzzles Anne. She also acknowledges that she doesn't want to join in their fun but prefers to remain as the onlooker.

Soon after, she notes that her father tells Harry to "stop," and she senses her mother getting tenser, telling her father also to "stop it." At this point, Anne feels confused, not yet having caught onto the idea that the mood has shifted, the playfulness turning to something darker. Once she realizes this, the fear ripples up Anne's body, and she becomes "more alert," the tension "building" to a sensation of fullness.

She wants "to see what is going on here," but no one makes eye contact with Anne. "I want my dad to look at me. . . . I want him to see the look on my face." With prompting, Anne asks, "Dad can you just look at my face? Turn around and look at me." The image of her father turns and when he makes eye-contact with Anne, she feels "glad that he's looking at me, because then he sees . . . what he's doing, it's scaring me." She sees in his eyes "sadness and concern," and upon asking him to stop, he does, leaving the image of Harry on the stairs crying. Though Anne goes up to Harry and tries to comfort him, Harry turns from her, leaving for his bedroom. Anne notes a sense of sadness in both her stomach and her heart area.

Without the closure she needs, Anne agrees to try to speak with her mom, though she admits that she doesn't "have much faith" she will "get much answers from her." When I remind Anne that this is the memory-image of her mother, Anne takes on an authoritative tone that hasn't yet been present in her language, stating, "I'm going to go ask Mom because she knows." However, before she addresses her mother, she recognizes that she cannot be five- or seven-year-old Anne; she must encounter her mother-image as adult Anne.

She finds that her parents are in the memory-image kitchen, a beloved space for Anne, who notes feeling "happy to be there in this setting; there are a lot of wonderful things in the house." Still speaking with authority, she tells her father that she's going to ask her mother some difficult questions and "you can stay or you can go, but I'm going to talk to her about it"—with this, she's acknowledging the autonomy of the father-image. He decides to stay, making eye contact with Anne. As Anne makes her way to her mother, she collects the warm and happy energy from the space itself—touching the knobs of the kitchen cabinets, feeling them "really passionately."

When I ask how she feels about talking to her mom, she returns to a passive voice, using the language "I just feel. . . . I'll try. . . . I want to ask." Though Anne does bring herself into dialogue with her mom, her mother's response is only that of tears and the answer, "I don't know" to Anne's question, "Why is there tension between Dad and Harry?" Anne insists "there must be a reason," and her mother responds only that "Dad just always thought that Harry couldn't do enough, couldn't do what he's supposed to do." Because this doesn't feel like enough of a reason, Anne replies with questions of whether her father felt forced to marry Anne's mother because she was pregnant with Harry, or whether Harry was even her father's biological son. Her mother's only response is to cry, and that frustrates Anne, who eventually decides to turn these questions to her father.

Anne's passive language shifts back to more of an authoritative tone as she asks, "Dad what's going on? Why are you so mean to Harry all the time?" She struggles with the questions she wants to ask her father, ultimately asking the same ones she asked her mother.

Pressuring her father to respond, Anne believes her father is telling her that "Harry never treated him with respect . . . . he just never does things right." The response is painful for Anne, who feels that this does not warrant the consequence of her brother's life being shadowed by such sentiment.

As Anne sits with her father, she becomes aware that her father was treated in the same way by his father, a family pattern passed down. She now turns toward her mother, challenging her as to why she "didn't try harder." The images of her parents are passive, listening but without response. With prompting, she tells them that she's trying to "relieve the pressure, the tension" and negate some of the pain experienced by watching Harry "not want to be loved by us."

In a final movement of the imaginal remembering experience, Anne agrees to return, up the stairs, to Harry, finding him in a bedroom that they once shared. Before she goes, she lies on the kitchen floor, taking in its warmth, experiencing herself simultaneously as both the child and adult Anne. "It's funny because I feel like I'm adult Anne because I have the memory of being little Anne."

I am reminded of the philosopher Dylan Trigg's suggestion that "temporality and spatiality are fundamentally entwined, each implicating the other."[153] Indeed, he believed the material world shapes and constitutes our sense of self and the world. Our physical world experiences are embodied, and when we re-experience such events through memories we do so in part by reconnecting our own material self to the material world we originally experienced.

To this end, Anne then seems to gather both her younger and older self and takes them to Harry, believing he will be more receptive to her as her current self because, in their later years, he became more open to Anne and her love for him. She apologizes to Harry for what he has endured. At first Harry looks away, but upon second approach, when Anne blames her father, Harry begins to cry. "Tears are coming out" as if there is a release of the pressure, the tension that has haunted Anne. They hug each other, and she tells him, "I'm sorry that I couldn't have been there more for you. I loved you." The image of Harry responds, "Well it was what it was, that was the way it needed to be." The imaginal remembering session closes with all the members of Anne's childhood family in the childhood living room, where she can "feel the love between everybody."

When the experience ended, Anne immediately shared with me, "That feels like a resolve is there now." As you may recall from Chapter 7, *resolve* is derived from the Latin word *resolvere*: to unyoke, to loosen, to set free. It would seem then that something was set free during this experience. My belief is that Anne reached a point where she came to realize and accept that the way in which Harry was treated was based on a pattern passed down from father to son: the pattern of not being good enough.

There is something paradoxically quite moving about where this imaginal remembering session takes Anne. She held the memory as evidence of, and came to the imaginal remembering session prepared to uncover, some sinister family secret. Yet she found that the darkness shrouding this original event and the years in which similar experiences occurred, weren't the products of something clandestine. Rather, they were tragic outcomes of generations of a repeated, regrettable pattern. The answer was surprisingly simple, albeit sad. Let's return to this in a moment.

Anne also offered that during the experience, "Everything is just vivid." To return to the home, especially the kitchen, which we recall is a symbol of the transforming self, seemed to aid Anne's ability to imaginally engage the memory and find the fortitude to carry her forward. For example, she noted feeling the warmth of the kitchen floor as if the sensual experience allowed for a deeper embodiment of the imaginal remembering phenomenon. She was having "reluctance . . . of revisiting all that, and it was hard to come up against my parents. But to be able to go into that safe kitchen and see myself switch back and forth from child through adult, it was all good." The kitchen and the beloved sensations this space re-collected held Anne and encouraged her journey onward.

Anne noted the pivotal moment in which she could move fully into the memory as a psychic image, allowing the memory to shape-shift. In the original event, she had no control of the situation, but could simply witness something the young Anne saw as frightening. But in accepting the autonomy of the memory-images, she could "have Dad turn around and look at me, so it's like I did exist in that . . . I have an impact on this."

Research suggests that bystanders to trauma, seemingly the role Anne identifies with in this original event, suffer from a sense of complicity because they have done nothing to address the traumatic event.[154] Thus, it may have been liberating for Anne to have done, in the imaginal remembering experience, what she's unable to do as a young child. In the memory-image, she had greater control, shifting, as she mentioned, from child to adult.

This movement from child to adult, allowing her to engage in the memory-image from both perspectives, was critical for Anne. She noted, "I had to change into an adult. . . . I couldn't [approach my parents and Harry] as that developmental child who experienced the experience." She explained that originally the memory was "stuck there in the whole bubble, like a complex kind of thing." Originally, "there was no resolve . . . the kid was nervous about re-entering or doing anything different in the memory. But once I could [be the adult], I could step into it, it seemed to diffuse itself—the power of it . . . . so, it makes sense now." As the word *resolve* suggests, there must be dissolution, a breaking down. This comes to Anne because, through the imaginal remembering experience, "you look at the pieces," thus making it "not so overwhelming."

For Anne, "sitting through that session just opened up everything around the relationship with my brother and my dad in my heart," that place where Anne originally noted tightness. When she shared her original experience of the memory, "I was seeing through those eyes developmentally, not understanding, not from an adult point of view." The imaginal remembering experience "really just . . . helped me see it from that kid perspective rather than an emotional, shadowy perspective."

Anne came to recognize that the memory itself held onto the emotion of the child who "just want[s] it to stop." Once she experienced it (through imaginal remembering) from an adult perspective, she had more empathy for both her mother and father, whom, she realized, were in many ways doing the best they could.

This ability to be forgiven and to forgive seemed to come forward through both indirect and direct ways. That the image of her brother Harry returns her embrace at the end of the experience may have to do with Anne's and the Harry-image's ability to recognize that Anne was just a child when the original event occurred, indirectly suggesting that Anne has or was beginning to forgive herself. Anne directly acknowledged forgiveness of her mother and father. Of her mother, Anne stated, "It helps me not be so mad at mom; even back then she had six kids." It also helped Anne realize how she approached parenthood differently, ensuring open dialogues. In reaction to her father treating Harry as he did, Anne noted, "I knew it consciously, but for me to get in touch with that again at this level, it helps with the forgiveness of what he did to Harry."

Thus, for Anne, a shifting in relationship occurs with Harry and her father even though they have both passed. Anne believes that there's something that exists beyond this physical world. "I feel like they're watching and that possibly healing can happen on the other side as well." She noted in our follow-up call that she has been more aware of their presence. That they have both passed makes the imaginal remembering experience perhaps even more important because "when people die . . . you have these issues left unsaid or undone. I think this has helped a lot with that; helped finish and close that one incident with them." She noted:

> I think that their spirit is always with us in some way in our hearts or minds, and if you can bring peace to those places, your heart and your mind, in any way, it's going to benefit you, and who knows what it does for them? So, I do think it does affect us. They don't just go away, I don't think.

Even though both are no longer of this world, Anne has found greater peace in her relationship with them.

"It's a continuation of relationship with them. . . . They're in a different place . . . but the relationship continues." For Anne, resolving what she termed a "shadowy piece" of her past allows her to move forward; it "is helping with the energy exchanged between us," even if that energy is experienced spiritually rather than in the physical world. I wonder if it also allows Anne to move into a new relationship with her past self, that little girl who didn't understand, who was afraid, who wanted love for her brother, and who regretted her inability to change things. It seems that a mending comes to the relationship Anne holds with herself. The past self and current self heal together, ultimately for the sake of the future self.

Letting Go, Loving On: Francis's Story

Francis is a petite woman with dark hair, olive skin, and green eyes. She told me once that her mother is Irish and her father Italian: Francis seems to perfectly represent both aspects of her ancestry. We have known each other for many years but as friendly acquaintances, both of us sharing a love of yoga. From afar, I have witnessed her battles with illnesses and the loss of loved ones, and I have come to admire the ways in which Francis, despite difficulties faced, continues to meet life with warmth, courage, and deep curiosity.

When I asked her if she would imaginally remember with me, she was a little uncertain at first, afraid that she would be "wasting my time." I assured her that as far as I was concerned there could be no wasted time because whatever the work amounted to, I would find it meaningful—even if it disproved my running hypotheses. The truth is, I had been curious if imaginal remembering could deepen one's connection to the creative muse. You see, Francis is a very talented artist, and the subjects of her paintings range from lovers to boats, cows to hydrangeas. Regardless of what she paints, the work is evocative and seems to express the emotion of the subject whether it be animate or inanimate. She explained once that her hands are a conduit through which the creativity flows. To be sure, emotion flows through them, too.

She thought about my request for an imaginal remembering session for a few weeks. Then one day I received a message from her in which she shared that a memory had "popped up" and was something she was certain she wanted to work with imaginally. She was a bit worried it would be too short, too simple. I explained that it needn't be more than something she was drawn to and seemed to hold affect for her.

As she recalled it, the memory is nearly fifty years old, and when she saw it in her mind's eye, it was in black and white.

> We were living in Connecticut, so I was either four or five, maybe. And my mom was sick, and all the rest of the kids were at school. I just remember her. She did not feel well,

so she was in bed sick. And she just let me play with her
hair and play beauty parlor with her, and I kept brushing
her hair and rolling it in curlers and . . . just taking good
care and making her all pretty. And she was just so patient
and really felt terrible. And I don't know why that popped
up in my head. And I just find it ironic that now I'm in the
situation where I'm taking care of her. And that just hit me
yesterday, that I was like, "Oh," because I was thinking
about this coming up. And so that's it.

She explained that she had two older brothers and a sister who would
have been at school when the original event occurred. She also
shared her hunch about why the memory was coming up now for
her. "I'm not sure how it dawned on me . . . I knew we were going to
be doing this. And I'm sure I was trying to make sure this was the
right memory." Francis laughed and then continued.

I think what happened is I started thinking about my mom
[in the memory] being so sweet, and it just sort of morphed
into my mom being so sweet now. But then oh my
goodness I'm taking care of her now. . . she's in memory
care, and she thinks I'm her mother. And I don't do her
hair, but I'm just there. I talk to her every single day. . . .
The roles have reversed . . . I am caring for her. And when
she's stressed, she calls. Well, one day recently, I went in
there, and she was really afraid. And she said, "Alls I
wanted was my mother, and there you were." And I was
like, "Here I am." Yeah, so it's just interesting how
everything is. So that's how I'm taking care of her . . . not a
physical taking care of . . . definitely an emotional and
spiritual care.

Francis referred to the emergence of the memory as a weird twist as
if to suggest that life has turned back upon itself. In the memory, the
young Francis cared for her mother in the way she could, and the
loving embellishments of outward attractiveness seem to
acknowledge the inner beauty Francis saw in her mother. In the
original event, she mothered her mother in the way of a child. Now,
she mothers her mother, who is in later stages of a Lewy Body

Dementia, in the way of an adult daughter, supporting her and easing her emotional strife. Though her mother hasn't passed, she is slipping away.

In Chapter 4, we met Rachel who imaginally engaged the memory of her mother's attempted suicide. In the memory-image, as it was met in the imaginal, the daughter rocked the mother, bringing love and comfort to the fragile, childlike mother-image. In that image, the archetypal story of Demeter and Persephone surfaced, evidencing the fluidity of mother-daughter relationships. Here, in Francis's story, we see the same pattern.

We spoke more about her current relationship with her mother. Francis described her as a physically spry 80-some-year-old, still able to move about, still "physically vital." Yet she's different to Francis.

> She's not who she was. But she's also not less than, by any means. She's just different. . . . Her self, her person, her soul is on its way. You can just see it, almost . . . it's not just mentally not there. I can just feel her spark is not as much there. And I know she doesn't want to be here. She doesn't want to be.

She explained that her father had died unexpectedly in a car accident just a little less than two years before our conversation, and she feared that her mother was holding on for the sake of her children.

> Part of me thinks that she's hanging on. She doesn't want to go. I don't feel a loss, a sadness about it because I know she would be happier . . . I know she would be. I mean, I believe life goes on, and I think she's partway there. . . . I just feel like this is her soul's process, and it needs to take the time that it is. But I know the ultimate goal of where her soul will be, and I know she wants to be there, and I know she's not as joyful where she is . . . I want her to be peaceful.

I listened as Francis seemed to vacillate between emotions of wanting her mother—the "very strong, sassy, sarcastic, independent, and feisty little Irish lady"—back, while acknowledging that her mother was already moving on, somewhere. I watched as Francis's hands touched each other at pinched index fingers and thumbs, and then one hand moved from the other hand as if a gossamer thread was being pulled between them. She explained to me this was the way she saw her mother slowing letting go.

Prior to Francis entering the memory imaginally, I asked her how she felt in her body. She acknowledged tenseness in her heart, throat, and hands. As you may recall from previous chapters, the heart often represents the physical embodiement of relationships with those whom we love. The throat is associated to our voice and to the what and the way in which we communicate. The hands are associated with a good many things, including expressing outwardly what we feel and who we are inwardly. They are also associated to power, strength, and nuturting.

These qualities seem to be reflected in Francis's response to my question of what her hands meant to her. She described them as a source of nurturing—"I'm a toucher," she said, describing how she loves still to hug and caress her mother. I mentioned that her hands also seemed to be very expressive, complementing her spoken communication. She laughed and acknowledged that this trait of talking with her hands has been with her since she was a young child. "I'm just tactile. Like I always touch things. And I create with my hands." She took a moment to feel more intimately into her hands and noted, "I feel a lot of energy in them. Maybe it's not tense. Maybe it's just energy." Likewise, the heart felt "swirly," another reference to energetic movement.

Only her throat continued to feel tense, constricted. We agreed that we'd check in with these parts of her body during the imaginal remembering experience. They proved to be quite relevant partners.

After some time of meditation, she entered into the memory imaginally, her psyche placing her at an entrance.

I feel like I'm standing at the doorway to my mom's bedroom. So I'm watching, and it's a black and white image but lots of light. She's in bed. There're white sheets and

there's sunlight coming in from the window on the left side
of her bed.

Though Francis sits on a chair in my office, her body seems to
embody the self held in the memory of her mother's bedroom some
fifty years ago. I watch her movements as if I am also peering into
that same bedroom, that part of our home that symbolizes the most
initimate and vulnerable of our spaces.

The doorway threshold seems to invite Francis to move from a
physical reality into a psychical reality, and the black and white
perspective perhaps announces some kind of duality: timebound to
timeless; life and death; lightness and darkness; appearance and
disappearance. The sunlight streaming in from the window on the
left suggests illumination from a non-rational, perhaps more spiritual
or psyche-centered source. Francis continues:

> That's where I am. I have my crazy pixie haircut and a dress
> on with a collar and a bow. And I'm sitting on the bed with
> my legs crossed, and she's laying down. A light's coming in
> across the room from the window there as well. She has a
> round brush, a skinny one. She's laying there on her side
> with her hands, I guess, tucked under the pillow but
> diagonal on the bed so her head's near me. And I just keep
> seeing the curl. I keep pulling her curl. Just grabbing a
> section and curling it, rounding it with the brush. Going in,
> upward. And her hair's soft. Short, but soft.

I watch as her hands brush the imaginal curls of her mother's hair,
the methodical reaching and
pulling the brush through the
ringlets becomes visible to
me in my own imagination.
As she pulls the brush
through her mother's hair,

> Hair is incredibly potent. . . . One of the
> first ways we register transformation is by
> something we do with our hair.
> ~ Ami Ronnberg[155]

again and again, she notices that the curl, a symbol of what is bound,
begins to soften until it almost loses its shape. The part of Francis's
mother most representing her outward identity is shape-shifting as
the brush is pulled through it. What was once bound is letting go.

Francis notices that her mom "really wants to rest," so she agrees "that I'll be quiet, and I won't bother her, but I still want to brush her hair." This desire to stay present to her mother is felt in Francis's hands and her heart, but she also begins to notice other things around the room of the memory-image.

There's a mirror, like at the end of the bed on that wall. I don't think we can see us, though. Yeah, I can see my mom. She's young. She's smiling, actually. . . . She's a cutie. She was a very beautiful lady. There's other stuff. Which I guess would be behind the bed if it's reflecting. But I don't know what it is. It's just darker. . . . It's funny, I see her here where my hands are, but she's different in the mirror. Hair's done already. And she has these beautiful cheekbones, and she's smiling. You can see the cheekbones. So, it's also different, like it's a different image. I was just about to say I don't know the image in the [mirror]. And I'm not sure why I was about to say that.

I ask Francis to stay present to the image in the mirror, noting that the ego seems to be trying to make sense of how the image on the bed and the one in the mirror could be different.

Now I recognize her. Her expression changed. . . . She's just smiling. She has a hat on now. She's dressed up. It's so weird. She's looking back . . . I could be analyzing. She's looking back at herself. So, it's really not a reflection.

I ask her if she wishes to ask her mother-in-the-mirror-image what she sees. Francis replies that her mother answers, "Who I was." After some silence, Francis whispers, "I feel like she wants to turn and go." When I ask her how that feels, she replies, after another long pause, "It's okay. It's okay." And again, after silence and tears that trickle down her cheeks, "It's okay."

[The mirror is] seen as a symbol of the multiplicity of the soul. . . . it takes the mythic form of a door through which the soul may free itself 'passing' to the other side.
~ J.E. Cirlot[156]

I invited Francis to spend a few quiet moments, but she wished to talk about the experience. She asked me if this is what happens in an imaginal remembering session, finding it to be strange. I explained that it is normal to witness things in the imaginal that are quite astonishing to us from an ego-perspective. We checked in with her body, and she noted that her hands were heavy, her heart busy, and her throat was "not good." I suggested that possibly the feeling in the throat expressed something that still needed to be said. Francis replied, "I bet there is. I could feel myself…." She paused before asking, "Would it necessarily have to be to my mom?"

Francis then described to me that there was unfinished business with her dad. On the day he died, Francis had held back the words "'I love you'. . .How could someone do that?" Francis asked, as if to suggest she suffered from a sense of regret.

When Francis originally "put it out there" a few weeks earlier, listening for a memory that might wish to be imaginally engaged, "two intentions" arose—the one she had just worked with and this childhood memory:

> My mom was in the hospital for some reason. I don't know why. And my dad is sitting in this chair, and he's not a nurturer at all. And I was behind the chair, on the ground. And I was playing with the slats [of the chair] and I said, "I miss Ma." And he said, and I don't know if he really said this, but this is how I remember it, "Shut up…I miss her, too." And that was just—that's that whoosh memory. I mean, I could see the chair. I could see all that, but that's the words I hear. So, I don't know if that has anything to do with it. The stifle in my voice.

We discussed whether Francis would want to engage in this memory imaginally now—the work can be exhausting, especially when the memories carry a great deal of affect. She wasn't sure, so we returned to her body to check for clues. She mentioned that her hands continued to feel heavy. Her throat felt even tighter, suggesting to her it was important to engage with the memory. She did not describe the feeling in her heart. We took some moments for meditation before Francis entered this memory as an image.

She begins by describing the entrance to the memory-image, at a threshold with the activity to the left side of the room, symbols we recall from her first imaginal remembering experience.

> This is in color. And I'm standing at the doorway, and the chair is to my left. My dad's sitting in it, watching TV. [Silence.] I'm behind the chair. I don't know why. The back of it is wooden, but there's a green cushion. And I was just running my hands up and down the spindles on it. There's a little green tie. I'm not sure what that's attached to but there's a little green tie. And I remember being afraid. I know that chair slides. It's a reclining kind of thing, so my hands could get caught if my dad moved. I can hear the TV in the background. There seems to be a standing lamp next to the chair. But where I was, was sort of dark. [Silence.] The wood is soft. It's smooth and that little string had texture to it.

As with the first imaginal remembering experience, Francis's hands help her to be present to the memory-image when she describes "rolling the string in my hands," its *green* the only noted hue for a memory "in color." Francis also runs her hands up and down the wooden slats of the back of the chair where her father sits.

I consider that the chair which her father sits upon and Francis hides behind as well as the green string she rolls between her fingers may hint at the psychological foundation of the memory and the possibility of where the imaginal remembering experience may lead. The chair, like a throne, may symbolize a sense of authority and power. Green is pregnant with symbolic meaning to include the pole of death (rot, pus, slime, decay) to rebirth (the buds and blossoms of springtime).

As she does this she says, "Just got to be careful" for fear of harming her hands. We remember that Francis identified her hands as used for nurturing, the very opposite of the way she described her father, as "not a nurturer." His movements could harm a fundamental way in which Francis engages with and offers the beauty of herself to the world—regarding the safety of her hands, she must be careful.

Francis notes that she wants to speak with the memory-image of her dad but hesitates to, "hiding" behind the chair. She stays present, hands touching the wooden chair, and notes that the tactile sensations, in the imagination, help her to feel calm, but also "anticipatory." She is waiting on something—either "the right moment" to talk to her dad, or for her hands to eventually be crushed in the movement of his chair—exactly what she anticipates, she is not sure.

Though touching the chair helps calm her, it doesn't bring her the strength she needs to face her father who she sees as "scary." I ask her if something in the memory-image might offer her that strength and then her dog, Liza, arrives by her side. As she rubs Liza's ears, she notes that Liza is "not afraid to look at my dad." In Liza's eyes, Francis sees love. She also recognizes that Liza sees her dad differently—"Not someone scary. Someone who's sort of sad and alone. Not as strong as—or he doesn't want to be as strong." There with Liza, she begins to not feel afraid, but also recognizes that her dad "would be unable to comfort me. So almost like I don't need to" seek comfort from him. We check in with her heart and her throat, and they are better, the throat not as constricted. "I can breathe better," she says.

> Symbolically, to breathe is to assimilate spiritual power. . . . Difficulty in breathing may therefore symbolize difficulty in assimilating the principles of the spirit and of the cosmos. . . . the rhythms of the universe.
> ~ J.E. Cirlot[157]

She describes how she wants to tell the image of her father, "It's going to be okay." Finding that she has come around from behind the chair, she faces him and notices that "he's sort of curled in the chair." After some silence, she shares with me, "There're sort of two hims . . . there's the one that I would normally see" as well as "a sub-image of him, a ghost image of him curled up on the chair."

Though she wishes to engage with the "curled up" image of her father, she is "afraid." I suggest, and Francis agrees, to rub Liza's ears for strength. She soon notices that the fear is "starting to dissipate, and I could probably climb up there and just curl up next to him. The other one," the ghost image of her father. "He's looking down, not at me, but he's looking down . . . he seems smaller, sad." After a few moments of silence, she whispers, "I think I could go up there. Tell him it's going to be okay." It is hard for Francis to visualize this togetherness but she "can feel his arm around me" and senses that her father-image feels "afraid" and "regret."

I ask Francis what her hands would like to do. "I don't know," she replies, sharing "I love his hands. He has big hands." I ask how her hands are feeling and she tells me, "Comfortable, actually." She laughs, and then shares that they feel "awkward, but warm." Francis then focuses on the imaginal hands of her father. "He has nice hands. They're strong. They're big. They've got veins. Big ring. It's his academy ring." I watch as Francis looks down, her hands held open as if she is holding her father's hands in hers. "Powerful hands," she says. "He used to hit us with those hands, actually." After some silence, I ask Francis how the image of her father reacts to what she has said.

> He is sorry. He just doesn't know, and he is sorry. He's sad, and he just doesn't know. . . . It's okay. It's all okay. [Silence.] He caused a lot of hurt, but it's okay. [Silence.] And he knows that. [Silence].

I ask Francis if she can look into her father-image's eyes, but she shares that she can only see his hands. I ask her if there is anything she wishes to say to his hands.

> Probably a lot. They're beautiful hands. They are. But they don't always do the right things. [Silence.] They're powerful. But I want—I just want him to know to use it for good. There's energy in your hands. [Silence.] He's okay. He's okay.

I ask Francis how she is, and she replies, "I'm okay. I can feel it, and I'm okay. Yeah." Her hands are "good. They're peaceful. They're connected," and her heart and her throat are "good. Good."

Francis soon looked at me and shared, "That was weird, too." She didn't want or need the silence following the imaginal remembering experience possibly because she had taken the time during the experience to find her space, to move slowly, and to let the experience fully unfold. Perhaps, too, she wished to share with me how odd it was to her to engage with her memory in this way. She described it as a kind of

> journeying . . . like I was talking to my dad, like his higher self, actually . . . it felt good to tell him those things in this setting, I guess, because I could say something, and he would listen. Or I could say something, and I could get it out without having to worry about a consequence, or a response, or a reaction, so it was safe.

We are reminded of Rasputin and the conversation with his dad-image: a conversation that was always necessary but, in the imaginal, was safe and grounding. It is as if Francis's voice, too, finally could speak its truth in the safe container of the imaginal.

We sat there together in my office discussing Francis's experience. She felt as though each imaginal remembering experience was connected but also separate. Each shared the element of letting go. Yet the one with her mother is about letting go of her mother, allowing her to slip beyond the veil, leave this physical world. With her father, it is about letting go of an unresolved past.

> I was letting my mom go, which is weird. My dad's already gone, but I had to let go of—well, I don't know. I don't know. It's definitely unfinished. When my dad died, I thought, "Just got to deal, Francis. You just got to deal." So, it's good to revisit that. And it was good to revisit it, in a way, as an observer.

There is something quite valuable in bringing the current self into to the memory of the child. The child, as Francis shared, is innocent, but also lacks a "bigger picture in the world . . . as the observer, I could not only see the whole thing, but I could feel it from the perspective of me now."

There is less attachment and greater understanding, Francis shared, by experiencing the memory-image as an observer. "When I was the child, [it was about] what I needed and my fears. And then when I came around that side of the chair and I saw him . . . I saw him curled up. So, I could see it differently. So that was good. It was really good," because it invited a different perspective of her father and the memory itself. You may remember in Chapter 4 that when we approach an image in the imaginal, we approach it as the *observing ego*, that softened ego of the phenomenologist who carefully observes the image with a flexible and empathetic stance.

As the next several weeks unfolded for Francis, she paid attention to her throat and her hands. She was already aware but further appreciating the special quality of her hands, the energy and "vibration" that runs through them. She noticed that her throat "clicks and sticks" when she speaks and even sometimes when she breathes. She began a meditative practice to concentrate on the sensations of her throat, but she was also taking this knowledge out into her world, specifically with her relationships.

Weeks later, she explained to me that she still had so much left to say to her mom, but she understood that this "'mom'. . . is no longer with me." The "fears, insecurities" that she'd like to share with her mom, she holds back, aware that her mom who is physically present to her is no longer equipped to handle them. While this inability to talk with her mom makes her sad, Francis noted:

> There's part of me that knows the reassurance and answers are inside of me and not her . . . she is on a separate journey . . . I am on my own journey, and she is the catalyst . . . together but separate journeys . . . She is walking herself home, and I am witnessing it.

She thought of her dad and the words she held back before she last saw him. But what was voiced as "unfinished" business with her dad when we closed the imaginal remembering session seems to have resolved.

In the week that followed our work together she was on a trip to California and noticed a chair that was remarkably similar in look and feel to the one in her memory. These signs that we meet in the outer world that seem to complement what we are experiencing in our inner world, in our work with the psyche whether through dream analysis, psychotherapy, or imaginal remembering, these are what C.G. Jung called synchronicities.

For Francis, seeing the chair helped her feel that her dad is still present to her, reaching out. When I asked, she admitted that she hadn't given much thought to her dad since our meeting. She considered that during the imaginal remembering, "I was able to voice the hurt that I felt as a child. Something I never voiced then. And as an adult I didn't feel . . . the need to voice it . . . yet it was still inside of me." In allowing herself to say what needed to be said, she seemed to be arriving at a place of peace with her father and their shared history.

Though letting go has been a significant aspect of Francis's imaginal remembering experience, she shared with me that the greatest impact may be to not hold back what needs to be voiced, especially when it is love. This love is not just love for another, but "self-love" that comes when she's encouraged to "speak from my heart" rather than the ego.

She told me her daughter had recently voiced her needs—"asking for the moon," as Francis saw it—and the request had been met. Francis saw this as a sign that asking for what we need is valid and valuable.

She had the opportunity to do so soon after we'd met, sharing with family members something important to her that she'd been holding back. She believed the impact of engaging her memories imaginally may carry on through other relationships.

> I think this experience has been growing for me . . .
> realizing that I have a voice inside me that sometimes . . .
> needs to come out. Being mindful that it needs to come out
> as love, not in anger or fear, is the most important part. I
> think sometimes I've thought that speaking my mind was
> either unimportant or selfish... But I hope I realize now
> that there is a need inside me to express thoughts and
> feelings. If I do not express them I will hold them in my
> body somewhere. As they say, "the truth is inside" . . . I
> should let it rise.

Indeed, the truth does seem to live within us. It lives in the body as "clicks and sticks" in the throat. It lives in the "vibration" of our hands, and the "swirling" of our heart. I believe, too, that it lives within us as the psychic images of our memories that await our imaginative engagement with them so they, and our Self along with them, may "rise."

Returning to Them, Returning to Us

This chapter began with an acknowledgment that in the loss or the death of another, the self who is identified with that relationship lingers behind, often at the price of the whole self who cannot move forward. I raised the question, how do we become unstuck? How do we enable the parts of ourselves that linger behind to either come to a peaceful resting place or to carry onward? It seems to me that imaginal remembering is at least one technique to do just that.

In the stories of Francis and Anne, we see that by recollecting, *re-collecting* the images of both our past self and the departed one, we return to them so that we may help each move on. I do not necessarily mean that the *other*, the one nearing or beyond the veil, is impacted by our imaginal remembering experience (though Anne believes this is the case with her father and brother). I do believe that *the other who lives within us*—like Francis' father-image illustrates—as the image within our psyche that has been, is, and may continue to shape our self, does have the capacity to shift and to move on.

For Anne, by returning to this long-ago memory, this time imaginally and as the adult-Anne (the Anne made wiser by the experiences of her own life), she could help the child-Anne unbind the bound-up energy that darkens the memory, setting it free through understanding and then love and forgiveness. Indeed, this love and forgiveness belongs to Anne's father and mother, whom Anne came to realize were likewise haunted by ghosts of their past. But I also believe this love and forgiveness belongs to Anne, too, the young child who could do nothing and the older adult who knew not what to do.

In the story of Francis, we again witness the value of bringing our older self to our young-child memories. When we meet them in this way, we observe the images through the wisdom of our current self. This helped Francis to find the courage and love to engage with her father-image, an image she saw was also hurting and scared. From this, she could voice the pain he'd caused so that she could let it go. In opening herself to imaginally engaging with the image of her mother (whom Francis is in the process of letting go from the physical world), she is also learning to let go of her pattern of silence. Through the memory-image of her mother, and her work that followed, Francis realized that she holds within herself the wisdom and valor she believed could only be found in her mother. This includes a growing understanding that to love herself she must communicate what she needs to say, to speak the truth that lives inside of her and comes from the heart.

If we nod with even the slightest resonance for the Counting Crows' notion that "dreams are like movies," aren't we obliged to consider the concept that "memories are films about ghosts"? We re-collect these apparitions of our former selves, and those we've lost, as psychical images who present to us through our memories. When we meet and imaginally engage with them, we return anew to our departed and to our self who was in relationship with them. Like so, we are invited into a deeper relationship with those we've lost and the self we once were, the one we are now, and the one we are yet to be.

CHAPTER 9

EMBARKING ON YOUR OWN IMAGINAL REMEMBERING JOURNEY

When I set out to approach memory as image, I honestly had no idea where it would lead. There were many times I got stuck in doubt, changed topics of interest, or I felt so overwhelmed by it all, that I just shelved it. But something kept calling me back to the idea. I think that something was the stories of the people I met. I sat in their presence while they shared with me what was happening in their mind's-eye. I trusted in what the images shared with them, and sometimes I could swear that I saw and heard, along with them, what they were seeing and hearing. I have been asked what it is like to witness these stories: it has been an honor.

This, I believe, is the role of the witness or the guide—to hold these stories with care. Francis, whose memory shifted into something quite meaningful to her current self, repeatedly asked me if "this is supposed to happen." I had only to offer her that it did with others, was seemingly supposed to happen with her, and I found it amazing. I've never doubted the images that reveal themselves to those who have worked with me; and I think in return the images never doubted my and the rememberer's ultimate belief in them. The witness then, perhaps, acknowledges the realness of the experience even when the rememberer holds doubt. Perhaps what was "weird" at first to Francis can be seen by me as "beautiful" because I have the privileged vantage point of observing it at a distance, not directly experiencing the often-perplexing effects of working with our psychic material. I am an observer without being the *observing ego* that we discussed in Chapter 4. Perhaps, too, I trust in these experiences because I watch them unfold before my eyes, witness the astonishment of the one who imaginally remembers, and then (if I am so fortunate as to keep in touch with them) understand how the experience has and continues to shape their lives.

I do believe it takes courage to enter our memories imaginally, to accept what is psychically real when we are so accustomed to doubting anything that is not physically real. Every one of the stories I have witnessed in imaginal remembering sessions has left me humbled by the rememberer. Through their openness to the psyche, we imaginally engaged their memories. As individuals, each came to uncover something unique and valuable regarding what their memory offered when approached as a living image. Their personal stories stand on their own. In this final chapter, I aim to share some things I have learned, inviting you to embark, if you wish, on your own journey of imaginal remembering as rememberer, witness, or both.

Body as the Anchor

The philosopher Dylan Trigg wrote, "We experience place in an affective way. Our bodies orient us in place, and in doing so become the primary source of how we apprehend a given environment."[158] I take this to mean that the places existing as memory-images are intimately intertwined with the body that has experienced its surroundings sensorially. Aria, who was first oriented to only a

> The residue of a familiar place stored in the body hints at another dimension of the body's relation to its environment: Place becomes profoundly constitutive of our sense of self.
> ~ Dylan Trigg[159]

memory-place, became exquisitely present to her younger self (who lived in that space) when Aria became highly sensitive to her body's recollection of that lived experience. "All that sensory stuff that came in for me, it lives in me somewhere, as my memory." Indeed, the body seems to hold who we were in the times and spaces of our lives.

Rasputin's memory was of a repeated original event that held little movement or action. Rather, Rasputin intensely recalled the location of the original event, providing precise and particular features of the memory's setting. In the fine details of the space, the "musty smell," the "dirt or the dust," the drapery cords pushed aside, we peel back the images of that place to reveal a young Rasputin who, with no other descriptions than those of his surroundings, seems to invite us to witness his inner world, a reflection of his own sense of self.

Not only is the body key in re-experiencing the original event as a memory, but, as Julia argued, the body functions in deepening the current imaginal remembering experience because to physically move during the practice is "also part of making the sacred drama more real. . . . It's just re-enacting. . . . When we take that extra step to make a tone, or sing a song, or do some movement, it deepens it." It would appear as the body's dance with itself, an engagement with the past as an embodied experience of the present that may then become the original event of a future memory.

Angeline described the importance of the embodied experience of imaginally remembering as a different form of "re-framing it" because, for the most part, to reframe means to "do that intellectually." For Angeline, "to actually embody it, to go through it and to have the lived experience is to me a much deeper re-frame." It allows us the opportunity of "going back into the memory, and actually living it, and physically walking through it." Because, as we've discussed, memories reside in the body, embodying the imaginal remembering phenomenon allows the rememberer to go deeper into the memory. The present body is the foundation for reliving the past, especially in the case of imaginal remembering, which as an experience goes beyond the fixed parameters of the original event, inviting a renewed and imaginative experience to unfold.

Attunement to the present body is witnessed through the rememberer's actions and their words. When their bodies moved to touch the imaginal—when Francis imaginally brushed her mother's hair, when Lilly imaginally caressed the head of her newborn grandson, when Aria imaginally rubbed the sketches of the rosemary and forget-me-nots—the rememberer not only deepened into the experience, but the image itself seemed to deepen. As part of our body, the voice often changes as well. The voice holds a tone of wonder and is the body's vehicle for communicating, with active, present tense language, what the body imaginally senses. When our body is present to the image, the image is present to us, and we describe it as such. This is one reason we meditate before sharing the memory and before and after we engage the memory imaginally. This mind-body practice helps us attune to the wisdom of our soma.

Our body also safely grounds us. It reminds us that we are still physical beings though we are engaged imaginally. The body as anchor seems to allow us to go deeper into the imaginal because we are safely held in critical awareness that what is psychically real is not the same as being physically real.

This is an important point to stress: we are physical beings and there is a profound distinction between what is physically real and what is psychically real. We must live and function in the physical world: ultimately, I believe, our time spent in the imaginal helps us better do just that. The healing, understanding, empowerment, and creativity gleaned from our experiences in the imaginal are there to help us as we engage in realities of the physical world.

Our body, then, is a touchstone that ties us to the physical world while we engage with what can, especially at first, feel like the destabilizing experiences of the psychical world. When we leave the imaginal, we return, through awareness of our bodies, to our physical realities: the body which was there with us all along.

Image as the Sail

I continue to be intrigued by the way in which memories engaged imaginally originally surface. For some, the memories appear almost at the ready, as if they've just been waiting for someone to ask. For others, the memory seems to wait until the moment of engaging with them is at hand. Regardless, it's always felt to me that the memory needs to choose itself. Even in my own work, I cannot force a memory to be imaginally engaged. It seems that the image opens just when and how it intends.

Allowing or accepting the memory to choose itself is one way, I believe, that we honor its animate and autonomous qualities as well as its wisdom. The imaginal seems to know better than the ego which memory our psyche longs to engage. Aria (who had no obvious choice until after our first meditation during our imaginal remembering session) said, "I keep thinking that the psyche brought that memory for a reason. That was a really short period of time. It's very specific, and a lot of things changed in those seven months I lived there." Even though the memory didn't appear until we met to engage it imaginally, the reason for its revelation is unmistakable given the repeated pattern in her life of experiencing intimate brushes with death and subsequent rebirths of the self.

Julia also expressed this sense of unknown—"I honestly didn't know what I was going to do, which is also a really powerful way to be in the moment. . . . It's trusting." Here Julia seems to note a sort of innate wisdom that allows the ego to soften and the psyche to usher in the image that is calling.

In recalling Angeline's and Francis's stories, two memories seemed to desire engagement. In Angeline's case, her boyfriend Grant, the first man she had been in relationship with since Allan, appears in the first memory and then reappears in the second, the traumatic memory that she tended. She said, "A part of me wonders . . . will you get to the same place even though you use a different memory?" Certainly, that Grant's image arises from the beginning seems to suggest this: as Angeline's ally in the imaginal remembering experience, his presence from the outset is remarkable. In the case of Francis, though her two memories were different, they both seemed to point toward the same psychological need to let go, and the uncanny wisdom and strength that is held in her hands.

Submission to the memory's choice of itself is a powerful starting place to allow the memory-image to be the sail. The image, like a sail, pulls us forward into the seas of the psyche so that we may venture into the otherwise uncommon and undulating atmosphere within ourselves that we rarely witness.

There are other ways we can allow the image to lead. Even the way in which the memory-image invites us to enter can be powerful. Julia enters the image awakening, Francis stands at a doorway with energy coming from the left, Anne and Lilly stand at the bottom of a staircase that they must, eventually, climb. Aria begins in a kitchen, a place of transformation; Jennifer at a fire, an element of both destruction and creation. Where the memory image begins is no mistake or casual reference. There is much to be learned even in the wisdom of its opening.

But when we speak of image, it's not just what we see, as the term implies. In imaginal remembering, as you may recall from Chapter 4, we stretch the term towards all the ways in which we can *imagine*: what we touch and hear are also quite important. The way Angeline's imaginal remembering experience begins illustrates this— she describes in such an odd but quite illuminating term—"listening really loud" for sounds that might alert her to danger. Rasputin hears his father's wheelchair go by, inviting a long-awaited conversation. Francis's hands touch hair, wooden chairs, and her dog's soft ears, bringing her calm and strength, as do the kitchen cabinet doorknobs and linoleum tile floor of Anne's beloved childhood home. Even the scents of the family dinner help to better ground Aria into an emerging image and seem to explicitly call attention to her innate creativity, as well as implicitly suggest that life is a comingling of ingredients: sweet and pungent coexist.

Yet, we cannot fully experience our imaginative senses unless we become very attentive to the image. This seems to happen through a slowing down. The more a rememberer allows herself to slow down and fully experience the presence of the memory-image, often in a multitude of sensorial ways (touching, listening, smelling, seeing), the more the image reveals its wisdom. This was evidenced most explicitly in Lilly's case where the vitality of the memory-image emerged when she paused on the landing to hold the doorknob.

When the rush of recollection is softened into a slow, attentive approach, this invites a more available and intimate presence to the memory-image. In slowing down, Anne allowed herself to demand that her father-image look into her eyes and be mindful to the pain he was causing so that an opening could be made. In slowing down, Aria found her lost research and felt the pages of her journal, rubbing the sketches of the rosemary and forget-me-nots that transported her to her grandmother's land.

Further, by being fully present to the memory-image, by slowing down and allowing for a multisensory experience, rememberers notice objects and figures, details and qualities, they had not previously heeded. These observations are often fundamental to their experiences, both in terms of imaginal remembering journeys and their reflections upon them. Angeline found an ally in the drafting table who acknowledged her trauma and encouraged her escape. Jennifer withstood isolation, darkness, and the cold through the protective glade that was surrounded by massive trees and a roof of twinkling stars—through nature, she reconnected to her own strength and courage. Rasputin discovered the sliding glass door that freed him from the confines of the house and sent him into the nuzzling branches of the tall, sturdy, backyard tree. Liza, Francis's beloved childhood dog, came to offer Francis courage and calm as well as another way in which she might see her father. These benevolent and helper figures seem to support the self in its transformation towards wellbeing.

This slowing down and unconditionally inviting what is to be is both the work of the rememberer and the guide. I was particularly reminded of this when I worked with Francis, the artist. I hoped the imaginal remembering session might encourage a deeper relationship to the creative muse. As it turns out, it was about letting go, healing, and learning to speak her heart. Who am I to argue!

Through this beautiful experience, I observed the significance of my ego's softening and yielding to the soul's wisdom of knowing what really needed encouragement or insight or witness. I'm not suggesting that the creative muse isn't encouraged through the work of imaginal remembering. Yet, it does remind me that when we set sail with a purposeful intention for the work, we are sure to be humbled when we realize we've been tacking in the wrong direction, and in awe of psyche's course correction upon the seas of imaginal remembering.

Embarking on Your Voyage

So then where do you go from here? You could set this book aside, sliding it between two others that stand upon your shelf or clicking the carrot that sends it back to your e-book library. Or you could see it as an invitation to find your own ship and set sail upon the waters where the rivers of imagination and memory pour into the sea of imaginal remembering. If you wish to set sail, you will find in this last section a compass and a rough chart (for I do not know exactly where your journey will lead but only how you might guide your ship).

Of course, having read the stories and the guidance offered in Chapter 4, you already have a sketch of your imaginal remembering chart.

- You understand that first the memory is shared and discussed, listening for current life circumstances that might invite it to be imaginally engaged.
- You know that the memory is then engaged imaginally, and you have read examples of what that sounds like from the perspectives of both the rememberer and the guide.
- You are aware that, once the imaginal remembering session ends, the guide and the rememberer share a discussion, grounding the rememberer back into the physical reality as well as musing about any wonderment and insights experienced.
- You recognize that another discussion can occur later when perhaps the rememberer has had some time to allow the experience to "seep in" and wishes to share that deeper understanding with the guide.

But you may still be seeking some nautical markers, so to speak. Here are some that my voyages with imaginal remembering have taught me.

1. Find a companion for your journey.

- We have discussed the possibility of not having a companion, and we'll talk more about that in point 2. However, the witness / guide can be crucial in allowing us to deepen into the experience as well as assuring the sound return to our physical reality.
- If you choose a companion, this should be someone you can trust to both guide you during the session as well as maintain confidentiality when it's finished.
- This person can anchor you when the waters get rough. When we engage in the imaginal, we can be frightened by what we find there, and we may be tempted to

abandon the journey too quickly. Deeply engaging our psyche can sometimes feel unsettling, so you want someone to journey with you who will know when to help you feel grounded and safe, someone who can pull you back, through the body, to the shores of your physical world.

- This guide will also help to find your imaginal allies should you be able and willing to stay with the image.
- They should be someone who can help you open the sails of the image and move forward into the imaginal if you feel comfortable doing so. This means they need to honor the animate and autonomous images of your psyche, not questioning or directing them, but encouraging your engagement with them.

2. **Or support yourself as your guide.**

- To begin, when you see the word "guide" in these instructions, know that this guide may be the one that lives within you.
- Encourage that guide within you by abiding in the same way as another guide would—not rushing, honoring the images, and offering yourself as your own witness.
- Consider recording yourself and speaking aloud as you move through the imaginal remembering experience. This will allow you to document and then later reflect upon what happened (you'd be surprised by what you might otherwise forget!). You can immediately write down your experience, but there is something quite precious in listening to your own voice as you tell of the experience (for all the reasons we have spoken about).
- As you listen to yourself or read your written words, take the time to ponder what is both spoken and unspoken, written and unwritten. Listen to the way in which you speak or what words you choose to write down. Listen for how you are communicating to yourself. It may be that your psyche recognizes you as the witness and is purposeful in what and how to communicate.

- It still may be a good idea to let someone close to you know that you are engaging in this process. You don't have to offer them intimate details, but it's nice to know there is someone who, even from a distance, is witnessing the changes that maybe be occurring within you and your world. It also may help you feel safe and grounded, that there is this touchpoint to come back to when you have returned from the seas of imaginal remembering.

3. Begin with and maintain openness.

- Invite a memory to come to you rather than dictating a choice that may be more ego-driven. This may mean sleeping on it, literally considering new dreams, or watching for signs in your physical world that seem to point you towards a past event.
- When you begin the imaginal remembering session, your guide should ask, "What memory brings you here?" honoring the idea that imaginal remembering is psyche-centered rather than ego-driven.
- Meditating before recalling the memory, before the imaginal remembering, and after the imaginal remembering, is helpful in honoring the image and softening the ego (of both the rememberer and guide). During these quiet moments (three to five minutes works well), awareness of breath helps ground us to the body and return us to the present when the mind drifts, as it does, again and again.

4. Stay present.

- From the beginning, you and your guide should check in with the body as the anchor (this is another reason for the moments of meditation that precede each new step in your journey).
- Asking questions like, "What do you notice about the body?" or "What is happening in the body?" your guide can help you to heed somatic wisdom. For someone

who does not have a regular mind-body practice, the questions may need to be more pointed such as, "Let's scan the body: moving from your toes up through the legs, into the belly, through the chest, up the neck, and out the arms. Where, if at all, do you notice stuck places or spaces that seem to have more energy?"

- Your guide should notice and bring attention to movements that you make with or the affects that evidence themselves through your body. For example, as a guide, I might notice that you have drawn your hand to your mouth and say, "Feel your hand at your mouth—what do you notice about yourself or the image as you hold your hand there?" Or if you've raised your hand to your mouth and then removed it, I might ask you to repeat the gesture, holding it there and asking the same question. If it's an affect that I notice as your guide—your flushed face, your coy smile, your furrowed brow—I may ask you to notice this yourself and to deepen into whatever emotion you're experiencing that brings you there. A question from your guide that is open and inviting might sound like, "I am noticing that you are smiling. What, if anything, do you notice about yourself, or the image as you smile?" Or, "How does the image respond to your smiling?"

- Your language is also a gauge for whether you're present in the image or have moved to observing the memory-image as a relic of the past. If I am your guide, I will be listening to your language as present or past tense. When I hear you use past tense, I will help guide you back to the image with questions like, "What is the image doing now?" or "What do you now notice in the image? What do you see or hear?"

5. Slow down, don't rush.

- There can be desire by both the rememberer and the guide to rush for several reasons, not least of which is the fear of running out of time. The first adjustment then is to leave plenty of time so that rushing isn't a function of needing to wrap up! Imaginal remembering sessions may take two to three hours to fully unfold, including sharing the memory, engaging imaginally in the memory-image, and then discussing the experience.

- Other reasons we rush include being excited by where things are heading or uncomfortable with what feels like stagnation when nothing much appears to be happening with the image. As rememberer and guide, we need to soften our desire to see what comes next or to fill in what we sense as an awkward silence (especially for the guide). Often in these moments of waiting, something is coming into being. If we imagine the chrysalis of the imminent butterfly, we know we cannot rush the opening of its wings.

- We can soften our desire to rush by simply getting comfortable with stillness. As the guide, we can also do this by helping the rememberer to move more slowly through the image, inviting them to pause and multi-sensorially witness the image just as it is.

- As the guide, when we're soft and still, it seems that our psyche will encourage us. Rather than our ego driving us towards something we're curious about, our own soul seems to point us toward the journey of the rememberer's soul.

6.   Trust in the image and the process.

- This is perhaps the most difficult. To trust our imagination may stand in opposition to everything we've been told. Our imagination is a curious and playful thing, what artists and writers might dabble with, but *trusting in it*, well . . . Yet, the trust is paramount. We cannot move with the image if we don't first trust in it or its movement.

- We build trust by first having trust in each other as guide and rememberer. We both trust in the process and the imagination of the rememberer, and trust that the image, as the sail, will move us along.

- In practice, this means employing all that we have discussed: being attentive to the body, listening for being present, slowing down, and noticing the image in a multitude of sensorial ways.

- It also means allowing the imaginal remembering experience to not make sense—to be something inexplicable, at least for now. It means accepting that what we might otherwise call "failure" is a success, not because the experience has answered our questions but because we've had the courage to engage in it.

7. **Explore the symbols.**

- Many aspects of imaginal remembering experiences can be associated to our personal lives. When we pull the image through our current life experiences, it may make sense; it is important to look to our personal lives for these associations, just as we discussed in Chapter 4.

- But, as you also may recall from Chapter 4, there is much to be learned when we consider the images from an archetypal, amplified perspective. This work relies on resources. In the Resources section, you will find a few excellent books for better understanding the myths and archetypes that stand behind many symbols within memory-images. Consider going to the library and picking up books on Greek, Egyptian, Hindu, Judaic, Christian, African, Nordic and other types of mythological and religious stories. Explore actual museums that house ancient artifacts, and learn what scholars say about such symbolism.

- You may also use your search engine to find websites that discuss symbolism. Typing in "what is the symbolism of a ladybug" on Google, for instance, yielded 394,000 hits just now. As a cautionary note, not all websites are created equal (and many just repeat what you can find on other websites). I've noted some of the most reliable in the Resources section.

- Keep in mind that the best way of working with symbolism is through sympathetic resonance. This means that if you read the meaning of a symbol and it doesn't resonate with you on a feeling level, you're not wrong! Don't let what someone else tells you an image means supersede your own sense of its meaning. On the other hand, don't be too quick to dismiss the symbolic meaning, especially if it comes from a reliable source. Sometimes these meanings need to unfold with time and only make sense upon deeper reflection.

8. **Journey on.**

Soon after your imaginal remembering session, allow yourself to carry the experience forward. Here are some suggestions.

- Journal what came up during the experience including what you and your guide discussed. You may even want to record your session and listen to it (just as you might when you are your own guide).
- Write down your dreams that follow the imaginal remembering experience and consider how they may be related.
- Note synchronicities, those physical world encounters that seem to validate or brush up against your imaginal journeys.
- Draw, sculpt, paint, or write a poem or a short-story about your imaginal remembering experience. These creative endeavors seem to honor the images of our psyche and further share with us wisdom and healing.
- Return to the images. Perhaps there are still things left to be said or learned or witnessed. Allow yourself (with or without your guide) to meet again the images, acknowledging the relationship that's developed or deepened. This may occur during a quiet walk, a soak in the tub, or while you pull weeds from your flower garden—moments of physical solitude in which the image and you return, with reverence, toward each other.

- Share these with your guide and discuss what they might mean in connection to your imaginal remembering experience.

9.   Return home.

- Trusting in the imaginal remembering experience means trusting that we will and must return to our physical realities: the imagination is a beautiful place but not somewhere we can live out our lives.

Returning home is, I believe, the most important aspect of imaginal remembering. Perhaps the greatest gift of working in and with the imaginal is that we're better equipped to fully become the self we are, the one that lives in the physical world. Not every experience may immediately or clearly point us back to how we adjust to or deepen in our present physical reality, but we are physical beings, here on this planet for our own reasons and purpose. Imaginal remembering helps us journey backward to move forward, all the while illuminating where we are right now: the place of our soul.

I wish you well on your journey, fellow sailor of the soul.

SELECT SYMBOL, MYTH, AND FOLKLORE RESOURCES

Books on Symbolism

- Cirlot, J.E. (2014). *A dictionary of symbols* (2nd ed.). New York, NY: Welcome Rain.
- Hillman, J. (1997). *Dream animals*. San Francisco, CA: Chronical Books.
- Lake-Thom, B. (1997). *Spirits of the earth: A guide to Native American nature symbols, stories and ceremonies*. New York, NY: Penguin.
- Ronnberg, A. (Ed.). (2010). *The book of symbols*. Cologne, Germany: Taschen Press.
- Chevalier, J. and Gheerbrant, A. (1994). In J. Buchanan-Brown (Trans.), *A dictionary of symbols*. Cambridge, MA: Oxford.

Websites on Symbolism

- ARAS (n.d.). The archive for research in archetypal symbolism. Retrieved from https://aras.org/ (paywall)
- Louvre (n.d.). The Louvre museum website. Retrieved from louvre.fr/en
- Warburg Institute (n.d.). The Warburg Institute is the premier institute in the world for the study of cultural history and the

role of images in culture. Retrieved from
http://warburg.sas.ac.uk/

Books on Myths, Religions, and Fairy Tales

- Birrell, A. (1993). *Chinese mythology: An introduction.* Baltimore, MD: Johns Hopkins University Press.
- Colum, P. (1996). *Nordic gods and heroes.* New York, NY: Dover Publications.
- D'Aulaire, I. & D'Aulaire, E. (2003). *D'Aulaire's book of Greek myths.* New York, NY: Random House. (Original work published in 1962)
- Eberhard, W. (1965). *Folktales of China.* Chicago, IL: University of Chicago Press.
- Hillman, J. (2007). *Mythic figures.* Putnam, CT: Spring.
- Homer, (2006). In C. Boer's (Trans.), *The Homeric hymns.* Kingston, Rhode Island: Asphodel Press. (Original work published in 1970)
- Otto, W. F. (1954). *The Homeric gods: The spiritual significance of Greek religions* (M. Hadas, Trans.). New York, NY: Pantheon Books.
- Paris, G. (1986). *Pagan meditations: The worlds of Aphrodite, Artemis, and Hestia.* Putnam, CT: Spring Publications.
- Paris, G. (2003). *Pagan grace; Dionysus, Hermes, and Goddess Memory in daily life.* Putnam, CT: Spring Publications.
- Peldmann, S. (Ed.). (1965). *The storytelling stone: Traditional Native American myths and tales.* New York, NY: Dell Publishing.
- Scheub, H. (2000). *A dictionary of African mythology.* New York, NY: Oxford University Press.
- Shaw, M. (2011). *A branch from the lightening tree: Ecstatic myth and the grace in wildness.* Ashland, OR: White Cloud Press.
- Sturluson, S. (1954). In J. I. Young (Trans.), *The prose of Edda of Snorri Sturluson: Tales from Norse mythology.* Cambridge, England: Bowes & Bowes.
- Tatar, M. (2003). *The hard facts of the Grimms' fairy tales.* Princeton, NJ: Princeton University Press.

IMAGINAL REMEMBERING193

- von Franz, M-L. (1996). *The interpretation of fairy tales.* Boston, MA: Shambhala Publications.
- Zimmer, H.R. (1972). In J. Campbell (Ed.), *Myths and symbols in Indian art and civilization.* Princeton, NJ: Princeton University Press.
- Zipes, J.D. (Ed.). (2000). *The Oxford companion to fairy tales.* New York, NY: Oxford University Press.

Websites on Myths and Fairy Tales

- Ashliman, D. L. (n.d.) The Grimm Brothers' children's and household tales (Grimm's Fairy Tales). Retrieved from http://www.pitt.edu/~dash/grimmtales.html
- Crane. G. (n.d.). Perseus digital library. An evolving digital library with information and a database of art and archaeology images.
  Retrieved from http://www.perseus.tufts.edu/hopper/
- Theoi (n.d.). Encyclopedia of Greek gods, spirits, monsters. Retrieved from
  http://www.theoi.com/Ouranios/Hestia.html

NOTES

1. Ronnberg, A. (Ed.). (2010). *The book of symbols.* Cologne, Germany: Taschen Press, 236.
2. Aizenstat, S. (2003). *What is dreamtending?* Retrieved from http://www.dreamtending.com/dreamtending.pdf
3. Jung, C. G. (1983). Alchemical studies. In R. F. C. Hull (Trans.), *The collected works of C. G. Jung* (2nd ed.). (Vol. 13). Princeton, NJ: Princeton University Press. (Original work published 1957), 50.
4. Fleckner, U. (Ed.) (1999). *The treasure chest of Mnemosyne: Selected texts on memory theory from Plato to Derrida.* Dresden, Germany: Verlag der Kunst.
5. Coward, H. (2002). *Yoga and psychology: Language, memory, and mysticism.* Albany, NY: State University of New York Press.
6. Schacter, D. L. (1996). *Searching for memory: The brain, the mind, and the past.* New York, NY: Basic Books, 6.
7. Schacter, D. L. (1996). *Searching for memory: The brain, the mind, and the past.* New York, NY: Basic Books, 66.
8. Kandel, E. R. (2006). *In search of memory: The emergence of a new science of mind.* New York, NY: Norton.
9. Baddeley, A. (2009). Autobiographical memory. In A. Baddeley, M. W. Eysenck, & M.C. Anderson (Eds.), *Memory* (pp. 137-162). New York, NY: Psychology Press.
10. Schacter, D. L. (1996). *Searching for memory: The brain, the mind, and the past.* New York, NY: Basic Books.
11. Wheeler, M. A., Stuss, D. T., & Tulving, E. (1997). Toward a theory of episodic memory: The frontal lobes and autonoetic

consciousness. *Psychological Bulletin, 121*(3), 331-334. doi:10.1037/0033-2909.121.3.331.

12. Klein, S. B. (2015). What memory is. *Wires Cognitive Science, 6*(1), 1-38. doi:10.1002/wcs.1333, 17.

13. Klein, S. B. (2015). What memory is. *Wires Cognitive Science, 6*(1), 1-38. doi:10.1002/wcs.1333.

14. Conway, M. A. (2005). Memory and the self. *Journal of Memory and Language. 53*(4), 594-628. doi:10.1016/j.jml.2005.08.005

15. Schacter, D. L. (1996). *Searching for memory: The brain, the mind, and the past.* New York, NY: Basic Books.

16. Baddeley, A. (2009). Autobiographical memory. In A. Baddeley, M. W. Eysenck, & M.C. Anderson (Eds.), *Memory* (pp. 137-162). New York, NY: Psychology Press.

17. Baddeley, A. (2009). Episodic memory: Organizing and remembering. In A. Baddeley, M. W. Eysenck, & M. C. Anderson (Eds.), *Memory* (pp. 93-112). New York, NY: Psychology Press.

18. Conway, M. A., & Pleydell-Pearce, C. W. (2000). The construction of autobiographical memories in the self-memory system. *Psychological Review, 107*(2), 261-288. doi:10.1037/0033-295X.107.2.261

19. Conway, M. A. (2005). Memory and the self. *Journal of Memory and Language. 53*(4), 594-628. doi:10.1016/j.jml.2005.08.005, 596.

20. Damasio, A. (2010). *Self comes to mind: Constructing the conscious brain.* New York, NY: Pantheon, 8.

21. Damasio, A. (2010). *Self comes to mind: Constructing the conscious brain.* New York, NY: Pantheon, 308 and 315.

22. Sheldrake, R. (1995). *The presence of the past: The habits of nature.* Rochester, VT: Park Street Press, 371.

23. Kandel, E. R. (2006). *In search of memory: The emergence of a new science of mind.* New York, NY: Norton.

24. Sheldrake, R. (1995). *The presence of the past: The habits of nature.* Rochester, VT: Park Street Press.

25. Bohm, D. (2003). The enfolding-unfolding universe and consciousness. In L. Nichol (Ed.), *The essential David Bohm* (pp. 78-138). New York, NY: Routledge. (Original work published 1980)

26. Bohm, D. (2003). The causal-ontological interpretation and implicate orders. In L. Nichol (Ed.), *The essential David Bohm* (pp. 183-197). New York, NY: Routledge. (Original work published 1987)

27. Aristotle (1999). On memory and remembering. In U. Fleckner (Ed.), *The treasure chest of Mnemosyne: Selected texts on memory theory from Plato to Derrida* (pp. 34-43). Dresden, Germany: Verlag der Kunst, 36.

28. Corbin, H. (1977). Prologue. In N. Pearson (Trans.), *Spiritual body and celestial earth* (pp. xxi-xxix). Princeton, NJ: Princeton University Press. (Original work published 1960), xxix.

29. Corbin, H. (1977). Prologue. In N. Pearson (Trans.), *Spiritual body and celestial earth* (pp. xxi-xxix). Princeton, NJ: Princeton University Press. (Original work published 1960), xxix.

30. Freud, S. (1899). Screen memories. *Freud: Complete works.* Retrieved from http://staferla.free.fr/ Freud/Freud%20complete%20Works.pdf, 208.

31. Schacter, D. L. (1996). *Searching for memory: The brain, the mind, and the past.* New York, NY: Basic Books, 277.

32. Casey, E. S. (1991). *Spirit and soul: Essays in philosophical psychology.* Dallas, TX: Spring.

33. Durand, G. (2000). Exploration of the imaginal. In B. Sells (Ed.), *Working with images: The theoretical base of archetypal psychology* (pp. 53-69). Woodstock, CT: Spring. (Original work published 1971)

34. Casey, E. S. (1991). *Spirit and soul: Essays in philosophical psychology.* Dallas, TX: Spring.

35. Bergson, H. (1959). *Matter and memory* (N. M. Paul and W. S. Palmer, Trans.). New York, NY: Anchor. (Original work published 1896)

36. Casey, E. S. (1991). *Spirit and soul: Essays in philosophical psychology.* Dallas, TX: Spring, 113.

37. Hillman, J. (1992). *Re-visioning psychology.* New York, NY: Harper and Row, 23.

38. Aizenstat, S. (2003). *The living image.* Retrieved from http://www.Dream Tending.com/articles.html

39. Aizenstat, S. (2011). *Dream tending: Awakening the healing power of dreams.* New Orleans, LA: Spring Journal.

198 DAPHNE DODSON

40. Hillman, J. (1979). *The dream and the underworld.* New York, NY: HarperPerennial.
41. Hillman, J. (2009). *Healing fiction.* Putnam, CT: Spring. (Original work published 1983)
42. Hillman, J. (1992). *Re-visioning psychology.* New York, NY: Harper and Row, 62.
43. Hillman, J. (2009). *Healing fiction.* Putnam, CT: Spring. (Original work published 1983)
44. Damasio, A. (2010). *Self comes to mind: Constructing the conscious brain.* New York, NY: Pantheon.
45. Sheldrake, R. (1995). *The presence of the past: The habits of nature.* Rochester, VT: Park Street Press.
46. Jung, C. G. (1977). Two essays on analytical psychology. In R. F. C. Hull (Trans.), *The collected works of C. G. Jung* (2nd ed.). (Vol. 7). Princeton, NJ: Princeton University Press. (Original work published 1928), 77.
47. Jung, C. G. (1989). *Memories, dreams, reflections.* New York, NY: Vintage. (Original work published 1961), 183.
48. Jung, C. G. (1977). Two essays on analytical psychology. In R. F. C. Hull (Trans.), *The collected works of C. G. Jung* (2nd ed.). (Vol. 7). Princeton, NJ: Princeton University Press. (Original work published 1928), 145.
49. Hillman, J. (2009). *Healing fiction.* Putnam, CT: Spring. (Original work published 1983), 75.
50. Hillman, J. (1992). *Re-visioning psychology.* New York, NY: Harper and Row, 3.
51. Otto, R. (1958). *The idea of holy: An inquiry into the non-rational factor in the idea of the divine and its relation to the irrational* (J. W. Harvey, Trans.). New York, NY: Oxford University Press.
52. Corbett, L. (2005). *The religious function of the psyche.* New York, NY: Routledge. (Original work published 1996)
53. Corbett, L. (2005). *The religious function of the psyche.* New York, NY: Routledge. (Original work published 1996), 16.
54. Schacter, D. L. (1996). *Searching for memory: The brain, the mind, and the past.* New York, NY: Basic Books, 277.
55. Damasio, A. (2010). *Self comes to mind: Constructing the conscious brain.* New York, NY: Pantheon.
56. Rubin, D. C. (Ed). (1988). *Autobiographical memory.* New York, NY: Cambridge University Press.

57. Deloria, V. (2009). *C. G. Jung and the Sioux traditions: Dreams, visions, nature, and the primitive.* New Orleans, LA: Spring Journal Books, 194.

58. Deloria, V. (2009). *C. G. Jung and the Sioux traditions: Dreams, visions, nature, and the primitive.* New Orleans, LA: Spring Journal Books, 194.

59. Maher, P. (2007). *Kerouac: His life and work.* Lanham, MD: Taylor Trade.

60. Hillman, J. (1979). *The dream and the underworld.* New York, NY: HarperPerennial.

61. Casey, E. S. (1991). *Spirit and soul: Essays in philosophical psychology.* Dallas, TX: Spring.

62. Aizenstat, S. (2011). *Dream tending: Awakening the healing power of dreams.* New Orleans, LA: Spring Journal, 59.

63. Bachelard, G. (1994). *The poetics of space: The classic look at how we experience intimate places* (M. Jolas, Trans.). Boston, MA: Beacon Press. (Original work published 1958)

64. Moran, D. (2000). *Introduction to phenomenology.* New York, NY: Routledge.

65. Jung, C. G. (1969). Psychology and religion: West and east. In G. Adler & R. F. C. Hull (Trans.), *The collected works of C. G. Jung* (2nd ed.). (Vol. 11). Princeton, NJ: Princeton University Press. (Original work published 1938), 544.

66. Watkins, M. (2005). *Invisible guests: The development of imaginal dialogues.* Woodstock, CT: Spring. (Original work published 1990)

67. Watkins, M. (2005). *Invisible guests: The development of imaginal dialogues.* Woodstock, CT: Spring. (Original work published 1990), 124-125.

68. Hillman, J. (2000). Image-sense. In B. Sells (Ed.), *Working with images: The theoretical base of archetypal psychology* (pp. 171-185). Woodstock, CT: Spring. (Original work published 1979)

69. Hillman, J. (2000). Image-sense. In B. Sells (Ed.), *Working with images: The theoretical base of archetypal psychology* (pp. 171-185). Woodstock, CT: Spring. (Original work published 1979), 176.

70. Jung, C. G. (1997). Three letters to Mr. O. In J. Chodorow (Ed.), *Jung on active imagination* (pp. 163-165). Princeton, NJ: Princeton University Press. (Original work published 1947), 164.

71. Watkins, M. (1984). *Waking dreams*. Dallas, TX: Spring. (Original work published 1976)

72. Johnson, R. A. (1986). *Inner work: Using dreams and active imagination for personal growth*. San Francisco, CA: HarperSanFrancisco.

73. Deloria, V. (2009). *C. G. Jung and the Sioux traditions: Dreams, visions, nature, and the primitive*. New Orleans, LA: Spring Journal Books.

74. Corbett, L. (2005). *The religious function of the psyche*. New York, NY: Routledge. (Original work published 1996)

75. Aizenstat, S. (2011). *Dream tending: Awakening the healing power of dreams*. New Orleans, LA: Spring Journal, 8.

76. Aizenstat, S. (2011). *Dream tending: Awakening the healing power of dreams*. New Orleans, LA: Spring Journal, 7.

77. Aizenstat, S. (2011). *Dream tending: Awakening the healing power of dreams*. New Orleans, LA: Spring Journal, 51.

78. Aizenstat, S. (2011). *Dream tending: Awakening the healing power of dreams*. New Orleans, LA: Spring Journal, 62.

79. Aizenstat, S. (2011). *Dream tending: Awakening the healing power of dreams*. New Orleans, LA: Spring Journal.

80. Freud, S. (2010). *The interpretation of dreams: The complete and definitive text* (J. Strachey, Trans.). New York, NY: Basic Books. (Original work published 1900), 121.

81. Aizenstat, S. (2011). *Dream tending: Awakening the healing power of dreams*. New Orleans, LA: Spring Journal.

82. Johnson, R. A. (1986). *Inner work: Using dreams and active imagination for personal growth*. San Francisco, CA: HarperSanFrancisco.

83. Jung, C. G. (2011). On the nature of dreams. In R. F. C. Hull (Trans.), *Dreams* (pp. 67-83). Princeton, NJ: Princeton University Press. (Original work published 1948)

84. Cirlot, J.E. (2014). *A dictionary of symbols* (2nd ed.). New York, NY: Welcome Rain.

85. Johnson, R. A. (1986). *Inner work: Using dreams and active imagination for personal growth*. San Francisco, CA: HarperSanFrancisco, 63.

86. Aizenstat, S. (2011). *Dream tending: Awakening the healing power of dreams*. New Orleans, LA: Spring Journal.

87. Corbett, L. (2005). *The religious function of the psyche.* New York, NY: Routledge. (Original work published 1996), 118-119.

88. Johnson, R. A. (1986). *Inner work: Using dreams and active imagination for personal growth.* San Francisco, CA: HarperSanFrancisco.

89. Hillman, J. (1992). *Re-visioning psychology.* New York, NY: Harper and Row.

90. Jung, C. G. (2009). In S. Shamdasani (Ed.), and M. Kyburz, J. Peck, and S. Shamdasani (Trans.), *The red book: Liber novus.* New York, NY: Norton.

91. Jung, C. G. (1989). *Memories, dreams, reflections.* New York, NY: Vintage. (Original work published 1961), 173.

92. Jung, C. G. (1989). *Memories, dreams, reflections.* New York, NY: Vintage. (Original work published 1961), 173-174.

93. Jung, C. G. (1973). On the nature of the psyche. In R. F. C. Hull (Trans.), *The collected works of C. G. Jung* (Vol. 8). Princeton, NJ: Princeton University Press. (Original work published 1960).

94. Hillman, J. (2009). *Healing fiction.* Putnam, CT: Spring. (Original work published 1983), 73.

95. Hillman, J. (2009). *Healing fiction.* Putnam, CT: Spring. (Original work published 1983), 72-73.

96. Aizenstat, S. (2011). *Dream tending: Awakening the healing power of dreams.* New Orleans, LA: Spring Journal.

97. Corbett, L. (2012). *Psyche and the sacred: Spirituality beyond religion.* New Orleans, LA: Spring Journal.

98. Trigg, D. (2012). *The memory of place: A phenomenology of the uncanny.* Athens, OH: Ohio University Press.

99. van der Kolk, B. (2014). *The body keeps the score: Brain, mind, and body in the healing trauma.* New York, NY: Viking.

100. Aizenstat, S. (2011). *Dream tending: Awakening the healing power of dreams.* New Orleans, LA: Spring Journal, 28.

101. Hillman, J. (1979). *The dream and the underworld.* New York, NY: HarperPerennial, 123.

102. Jung, C. G. (1997). Three letters to Mr. O. In J. Chodorow (Ed.), *Jung on active imagination* (pp. 163-165). Princeton, NJ: Princeton University Press. (Original work published 1947)

103. Trigg, D. (2012). *The memory of place: A phenomenology of the uncanny.* Athens, OH: Ohio University Press.

104. van der Kolk, B. (2014). *The body keeps the score: Brain, mind, and body in the healing trauma.* New York, NY: Viking.
105. Johnson, R. A. (1986). *Inner work: Using dreams and active imagination for personal growth.* San Francisco, CA: HarperSanFrancisco, 149-150.
106. Laub, D. (1995). Truth and testimony: The process and the struggle. In C. Caruth (Ed.), *Trauma: Explorations in memory* (pp. 61-75). Baltimore, MD: The John Hopkins University Press, 67.
107. van der Kolk, B., & van der Hart, O., (1995). The intrusive past: The flexibility of memory and the engraving of trauma. In C. Caruth (Ed.), *Trauma: Explorations in memory* (pp. 158-182). Baltimore, MD: The John Hopkins University Press.
108. Caruth, C. (Ed.) (1995). *Trauma: Explorations in memory.* Baltimore, MD: The John Hopkins University Press.
109. Levine, P.A. (1997). *Waking the tiger: Healing trauma.* Berkeley, CA: North Atlantic Books.
110. Levine, P.A. (1997). *Waking the tiger: Healing trauma.* Berkeley, CA: North Atlantic Books.
111. Levine, P.A. (1997). *Waking the tiger: Healing trauma.* Berkeley, CA: North Atlantic Books.
112. Aizenstat, S. (2011). *Dream tending: Awakening the healing power of dreams.* New Orleans, LA: Spring Journal, 28.
113. Levine, P.A. (1997). *Waking the tiger: Healing trauma.* Berkeley, CA: North Atlantic Books.
114. Levine, P.A. (1997). *Waking the tiger: Healing trauma.* Berkeley, CA: North Atlantic Books.
115. Cirlot, J.E. (2014). *A dictionary of symbols* (2nd ed.). New York, NY: Welcome Rain, 351.
116. Music, G. (2009). Neglecting neglect: Some thoughts about children who have lacked good input, and are 'undrawn' and 'unenjoyed'. *Journal of Child Psychotherapy, 35*(2), 142-156. doi.org/10.1080/00754170902996064
117. Music, G. (2009). Neglecting neglect: Some thoughts about children who have lacked good input, and are 'undrawn' and 'unenjoyed'. *Journal of Child Psychotherapy, 35*(2), 142-156. doi.org/10.1080/00754170902996064
118. Judith, A. (2004). *Eastern body, Western mind.* New York, NY: Celestial Arts.

119. Music, G. (2009). Neglecting neglect: Some thoughts about children who have lacked good input, and are 'undrawn' and 'unenjoyed'. *Journal of Child Psychotherapy, 35*(2), 142-156. doi.org/10.1080/00754170902996064

120. Ronnberg, A. (Ed.). (2010). *The book of symbols.* Cologne, Germany: Taschen Press.

121. Judith, A. (2004). *Eastern body, Western mind.* New York, NY: Celestial Arts.

122. Music, G. (2009). Neglecting neglect: Some thoughts about children who have lacked good input, and are 'undrawn' and 'unenjoyed'. *Journal of Child Psychotherapy, 35*(2), 142-156. doi.org/10.1080/00754170902996064, para. 9.

123. Music, G. (2009). Neglecting neglect: Some thoughts about children who have lacked good input, and are 'undrawn' and 'unenjoyed'. *Journal of Child Psychotherapy, 35*(2), 142-156. doi.org/10.1080/00754170902996064

124. Hillman, J. (1992). *Re-visioning psychology.* New York, NY: Harper and Row.

125. Casey, E. S. (1991). *Spirit and soul: Essays in philosophical psychology.* Dallas, TX: Spring.

126. Trigg, D. (2012). *The memory of place: A phenomenology of the uncanny.* Athens, OH: Ohio University Press.

127. Ronnberg, A. (Ed.). (2010). *The book of symbols.* Cologne, Germany: Taschen Press.

128. Ronnberg, A. (Ed.). (2010). *The book of symbols.* Cologne, Germany: Taschen Press, 576.

129. Judith, A. (2004). *Eastern body, Western mind.* New York, NY: Celestial Arts.

130. Ronnberg, A. (Ed.). (2010). *The book of symbols.* Cologne, Germany: Taschen Press, 128-130.

131. Ronnberg, A. (Ed.). (2010). *The book of symbols.* Cologne, Germany: Taschen Press.

132. Ronnberg, A. (Ed.). (2010). *The book of symbols.* Cologne, Germany: Taschen Press.

133. Ronnberg, A. (Ed.). (2010). *The book of symbols.* Cologne, Germany: Taschen Press, 296.

134. Paris, G. (2005). *Pagan meditations: The worlds of Aphrodite, Artemis, and Hestia.* Putnam, CT: Spring. (Original work published 1986)

135. Otto, W. F. (1954). *The Homeric gods: The spiritual significance of Greek religions* (M. Hadas, Trans.). New York, NY: Pantheon Books.

136. Judith, A. (2004). *Eastern body, Western mind.* New York, NY: Celestial Arts, 67.

137. Ronnberg, A. (Ed.). (2010). *The book of symbols.* Cologne, Germany: Taschen Press, 118.

138. Paris, G. (2005). *Pagan meditations: The worlds of Aphrodite, Artemis, and Hestia.* Putnam, CT: Spring. (Original work published 1986), 129.

139. Judith, A. (2004). *Eastern body, Western mind.* New York, NY: Celestial Arts.

140. Hillman, J. (1992). *Re-visioning psychology.* New York, NY: Harper and Row, 7.

141. Ronnberg, A. (Ed.). (2010). *The book of symbols.* Cologne, Germany: Taschen Press, 380.

142. Ronnberg, A. (Ed.). (2010). *The book of symbols.* Cologne, Germany: Taschen Press.

143. Cirlot, J.E. (2014). *A dictionary of symbols* (2nd ed.). New York, NY: Welcome Rain.

144. Ronnberg, A. (Ed.). (2010). *The book of symbols.* Cologne, Germany: Taschen Press.

145. Cirlot, J.E. (2014). *A dictionary of symbols* (2nd ed.). New York, NY: Welcome Rain.

146. Ronnberg, A. (Ed.). (2010). *The book of symbols.* Cologne, Germany: Taschen Press.

147. Ronnberg, A. (Ed.). (2010). *The book of symbols.* Cologne, Germany: Taschen Press.

148. Jung, C. G. (1989). Mysterium coniunctionis. In R. F. C. Hull (Trans.), *The collected works of C. G. Jung* (2nd ed.). (Vol. 14). Princeton, NJ: Princeton University Press. (Original work published 1956)

149. Jung, C. G. (1993). Psychology and alchemy. In R. F. C. Hull (Trans.), *The collected works of C. G. Jung* (2nd ed.). (Vol. 12). Princeton, NJ: Princeton University Press. (Original work published 1944)

150. Casey, E. S. (1991). *Spirit and soul: Essays in philosophical psychology.* Dallas, TX: Spring, 180.

151. May, R. (1999). *Freedom and destiny*. New York, NY: W.W. Norton.
152. Kuhn, R., (2004). The attempted murder of a prostitute. In R. May, E. Angel, and H. Ellenberger (Eds.) *Existence*. Lanham, MD: Rowman and Littlefield.
153. Trigg, D. (2012). *The memory of place: A phenomenology of the uncanny*. Athens, OH: Ohio University Press, xix.
154. Hollander, N. C. (2007). Scared stiff: Trauma, ideology, and the bystander. *International Journal of Applied Psychoanalytic Studies, 4*(3), 295-307. doi:10.1002/aps.102
155. Ronnberg, A. (Ed.). (2010). *The book of symbols*. Cologne, Germany: Taschen Press, 346.
156. Cirlot, J.E. (2014). *A dictionary of symbols* (2nd ed.). New York, NY: Welcome Rain, 211.
157. Cirlot, J.E. (2014). *A dictionary of symbols* (2nd ed.). New York, NY: Welcome Rain, 32-33.
158. Trigg, D. (2012). *The memory of place: A phenomenology of the uncanny*. Athens, OH: Ohio University Press, 6.
159. Trigg, D. (2012). *The memory of place: A phenomenology of the uncanny*. Athens, OH: Ohio University Press, 11.

ABOUT THE AUTHOR

Daphne Dodson, Ph.D., is a research psychologist, writer, and an excavator and curator of the stories of our lived experiences. She lives in North Carolina with her family.

Made in the USA
San Bernardino, CA
28 May 2018